Praise for *Growing the Top Line*

"Finally, a book from Cliff Farrah! *Growing the Top Line* is not to be missed. A fresh and simple framework to effective strategy by one of the greatest modern practitioners. A must read with Cliff's humble style throughout."

John Seebeck, Vice President and GM, eCommerce, CDW

"The combination of experience, discipline, drive, strategy, customer orientation, vision, trust, and execution are rare combinations in a person, but embodied in Cliff. This is reflected in the work he does as well as the talent he attracts and grows. Based on this alone, I would be surprised that anyone could resist the desire to read *Growing the Top Line*. Insights based on this type of talent are hard to come by."

Frank Soqui, Vice President and GM Desktop, Workstation and Channel Group, Intel Corporation

"I have known and experienced Cliff Farrah's approach to growth strategy for twenty-plus years. I can say with confidence that he is truly a national treasure when it comes to growing companies—his expertise is unmatched. *Growing the Top Line* is a 'how-to' for anyone serious about growth using a structured process and strategy framework that set the parameters for success. For defense contractors, this book should be required reading. Enjoy."

LTG Paul (Gene) Blackwell, Ret. US Army. Former Vice President, Business Development, Raytheon Corporation

"Cliff's systematic approach to framing growth opportunity areas for your business is worth the read. And yes—I'll buy 2."

Martin J. Curran, Executive Vice President and Innovation Officer, Corning

"Growth strategies can often be complex, which can lead to poor internal communication and misalignment on company objectives. Cliff Farrah's book, *Growing the Top Line*, is filled with useful insight and a framework that can simplify this process and clear the pathway for success."

Rami Rahim, CEO, Juniper Networks

"It is a rare opportunity when you get the chance to work with someone over a span of 20+ years and learn something new at each encounter. *Growing the Top Line* introduces Cliff's pragmatic approach to business growth and is a must-read for large companies and even growing start-ups. Too often consultants tell you what to do but it's a rare gem who rolls up his sleeves like Cliff does and helps implement the strategy he recommends. A 'win-win' for all!"

Sue Spradley, CEO, Motion Intelligence,
Board of Directors Avaya and Qorvo Corporations

"Cliff Farrah's book is a must read for any business executive looking to grow. Cliff's intelligent insights culled from his 30 years of experience are boiled down to a growth framework that can be used for businesses of all sizes and industries. And it is a book that bankers should require their clients read!"

Kevin Watters, former CEO Chase Card Services,
JPMorgan Chase

"In *Growing the Top Line* Cliff Farrah teaches how to think with an objective eye as you plan growth. He can seamlessly move from being an insider to an outsider. He understands how businesses operate and how to win in the market—a perfect and unique combination."

Sheri Dodd, Vice President and General Manager,
Medtronic Care Management Services

"Cliff Farrah has developed and road-tested a powerful approach to planning growth. Four simple questions and a repeatable process force traditional and non-traditional leaders to examine the universe of growth paths and prioritize them based on business objectives and expected ROI. While this sounds simple, experienced strategists know just how difficult this is. With *Growing the Top Line*, we are all better equipped to achieve our growth objectives."

Nancy Lyons Callahan, Global Vice President
Services Strategy, SAP

"I have been living Cliff's growth framework for the last decade at Beacon and am thrilled to see it come to life in *Growing the Top Line*. Cliff is sharing his simple yet comprehensive process for driving growth that has been benefitting Beacon's clients for years."

Oliver Richards, Chief Growth Officer and
Senior Vice President Healthcare, The Beacon Group

"With many years of strategy, innovation, and transformational growth work under my belt since Cliff introduced me to the Beacon Growth Framework, I am even more impressed with its comprehensiveness and utility in cutting through the fog of complexity to reveal actionable insight than I was in that first *aha* moment."

Rick Waldron, MOBE VP Strategy, Insights & Innovation

"For the past 20+ years, Cliff Farrah has dedicated his immense talents to better understanding the dynamics of company growth strategies. He is recognized as a true pioneer in the field. And now he's sharing with you his proven blueprint to successfully teach and execute growth strategy development."

Don Scales, Global CEO, Investis Digital,
author of *How to Lead a Values-Based*
Professional Services Firm* and *The M&A Solution

"I have worked with Cliff and the Beacon team for over twenty years while leading growth at Pratt & Whitney, Eaton, and Trojan Battery. Each time I have found Cliff's agile approach and insights to my business challenges to be on-point and actionable. Cliff's new book does an outstanding job of synthesizing their approach in a simple and usable way: a go-to tool for leaders charged with driving substantive growth."

John Beering, President, Arch Channel Retail, LLC,

"Cliff Farrah is one of the most innovative business strategists of today. *Growing the Top Line* is a must-read for every leader searching for the next growth opportunity."

Doug Fletcher, author, *How to Win Client Business*, co-author, *How Clients Buy*

"Cliff's strategy advice and business savvy are naturally in tune with human behavior, and he has an innate ability to understand—and articulate—how systems, processes, and people come together within an organization to create culture and drive growth-focused outcomes. Needless to say, I highly recommend Cliff as a strategist, a teacher, and a friend."

Michael Woodfolk, President, University of Virginia Darden School Foundation

"Cliff's success comes from an uncommon blend of data-based evidence, market insights and intuition, and highly developed skill at questioning key tenets which contaminate growth plans with unreasonable expectations and flawed assumptions. Any plan you build for growth must incorporate Cliff's approach, or you will surely be disappointed in the results."

Dave Murashige, Senior Vice President, Aria Solutions

"Once again, we've learned that hope is not a strategy...rather it is a focused and deliberate set of actions that focus on the needs of our business today and into the future. In *Growing the Top Line*, for the price of a good meal, Cliff Farrah gives us a pragmatic, useful tool as growth strategists."

Bob Roda, President and CEO at HemoSonics, LLC

"Cliff is a perpetual student of business strategies... dissecting the context, decisions, and outcomes they yield. He appreciates how well-developed strategies integrate decisions about markets and offers and structures, and he gets that modern businesses are challenged with a 'grow or die' reality. As a result, *Growing the Top Line* goes way beyond traditional strategy frameworks to outline a rich array of growth pathways. It's an indispensable roadmap for any business leader focused on enduring growth."

Tom Lattin, VP Product Planning and Strategic Technologies, ZT Systems

"I have known and worked with Cliff for 15 years, and seen firsthand how much Beacon's clients—many of whom are quoted here—value and have benefited from the sharp analytical framework (and focus on the real impact of any proposed solutions) described in these pages. As one of the founders of a boutique litigation law firm, I can say that *Growing The Top Line* carries lessons and insights for not just Fortune 100 companies and their consultants, but any professional services business that wants to not just survive, but thrive, in a challenging competitive environment."

Ray Austoras, Founding Partner, Arrowood LLC

GROWING

THE

TOP LINE

Four Key Questions and **the Proven Process**
for Scaling Your Business

GROWING
THE
TOP LINE

CLIFF FARRAH

WILEY

Published by John Wiley & Sons, Inc., Hoboken, New Jersey.
Published simultaneously in Canada.

For general information on our other products and services or for technical support, please contact our Customer Care Department within the United States at (800) 762-2974, outside the United States at (317) 572-3993 or fax (317) 572-4002.

Wiley publishes in a variety of print and electronic formats and by print-on-demand. Some material included with standard print versions of this book may not be included in e-books or in print-on-demand. If this book refers to media such as a CD or DVD that is not included in the version you purchased, you may download this material at http://booksupport.wiley.com. For more information about Wiley products, visit www.wiley.com.

Library of Congress Cataloging-in-Publication Data is Available:
ISBN 9781119779209 (Hardcover)
ISBN 9781119779193 (ePDF)
ISBN 9781119779186 (ePub)

Cover Design: Adela Smailovic
Cover Image: © The Beacon Group

SKY10026886_050621

To my bride, Kim. Thanks for taking a chance on a Yankee and saying yes those many years ago. I love all that you are.

Contents

Introduction

Twenty years ago, in the aftermath of the 9/11 attacks, I started a growth-strategy consulting firm called The Beacon Group. Like the business world, and the entire nation, we were in uncharted waters, the economy was a wreck, and we needed a path to recovery. I thought the name was fitting because, as a sailor, I knew that beacons were a critical part of safe navigation.

We were pioneers, breaking new ground in a field we called *growth strategy*. This was 2001 – there was no *Blue Ocean Strategy* or *The Innovator's Dilemma* books to guide us. No class on growth strategy was offered at B-School. We learned through trial and error by working with clients to help them scale, codifying the growth lessons we learned along the way, and by repeating them with other client teams.

Originally written as a training tool for our employees, this book began as a tool to teach consistency, a metric of quality in the services world. There are plenty of one-hit wonders in the business world, but we've always been focused on how the best of the best think about growth. Consistency was our goal and, in 2010, we began using our model to show clients how we developed our growth strategies. This model has been accepted as a standard with leading c-level strategy practitioners at Beacon's clients. This book contains interviews from current and prior leaders at major corporations, including Intel, Medtronic, CDW, Johnson & Johnson, Juniper Networks, Nike, Pratt & Whitney, Eaton, Motorola, SAP, Chase, Raytheon, the U.S. Army, Corning, EDS, Oracle, Crate & Barrel, Texas Instruments, The World Health Organization, General Electric, and Cisco, among others.

You'll also see learnings from successful entrepreneurs and operators of nonprofit organizations. Our model applies to every form of business.

This book serves two target audiences, although I think all growth strategists will find it valuable. Audience one is a first-time growth strategist. This is anyone new to planning the top line, or revenue growth, of a business. Perhaps they're an entrepreneur at a start-up or a freshly promoted employee in a Fortune 100 enterprise. If you fall into this category, this book was designed to teach you how to think about the development of a growth strategy and to give you the tools to build your own.

The second audience is the seasoned growth-strategy practitioner, whether you've been elevated to run strategy across your organization or you are looking to standardize a stale or scattered planning process. It is amazing how many companies follow a patchwork approach to strategy development and struggle to maintain quality of thought and consistency of information as they consolidate plan across their multiple business units around the world.

The past 30 years have been a wonderful journey, and I'm grateful to have had opportunities to serve clients around the world as they built and executed their growth strategies. This book shares what I've learned throughout my career, but especially what we've learned at Beacon, completing over 1,500 projects in the past 20 years for our global client base.

Please read this book more than once. I've tried to keep the tone conversational, but the message is layered and takes some consideration to fully absorb. The stories, the process, the method are all things that, as you gain experience, you'll find you can revisit to find learnings that you missed when you read it the first time.

Growth Strategy: What It Is and Why Companies Fail at It

Harrison sat in front of his computer, looking at but not seeing the monitor. His brain was racing, and he hadn't slept well in over a week. A former engineer, Harrison had been put on a management development rotation. So far, he'd worked in product development, manufacturing, sales, and now was in a product marketing role. Always a producer for his team, this was an entirely new environment for him. He had done some training on marketing, but it was mid-January, and he had been given the charter to lead the development of the strategy for his product line with a briefing due in 8 weeks for review with the business unit leadership.

It was overwhelming – where to begin? He had last year's plan, and a template to fill out, but it felt wrong – formulaic, stale, checking the box. Who cared about market segment share, or average sales price, or all the other tables that he had to fill out? He knew what it meant to design a product and manufacture it and knew that both departments were stretched thin. He felt the challenge of selling something new as the company had a retiring sales force and a new requirement for a new "solution" sale. In his gut, he felt that the reality of feet on the street didn't line up with these forms that the company had used for the past decade. His boss told him to just update for this year's plan, but rather than mailing it in, he felt the awesome responsibility of doing a good job.

If you work in the corporate world, at some point you will be or have been Harrison. And you were right to feel the disconnect between what you knew the real challenges of the job to be and the traditional annual planning document you were given.

When you mention growth strategy, a few different reactions occur. If you are telling your friends what you do, their eyes glaze over. If you are being told you have a new role, you may panic a bit. If you are the one letting people know they are now responsible for developing it, you may be a bit concerned about what you will get back from them.

Growth strategy development is the application of strategic thought to the challenge of growth. In its best form, it clearly articulates how you are going to achieve an objective. What you will do, who will do it, when it will occur, and why it is necessary to reach your goal. It reflects the strengths and weaknesses of your organization, the market landscape you will compete in, the adversaries you face, and the resources you have.

In the past 30 years, I've been lucky enough to work with the best of the best at Fortune 200 clients in healthcare, defense, financial services, software, hardware, professional services, industrials, pharma, consumer goods, technology, energy, education, and retail.

There are several key learnings that emerge when I look back on their growth strategy practices.

1. Everyone has a slightly different approach, although the very best have a structured, teachable, repeatable methodology.
2. If you "know," you know that it's all about the team that is executing.
3. There are core market elements universally assessed by the best of the best.
4. New business models have become recognized as disruptive and powerful tools.
5. Where you play geographically matters.
6. Timing is everything.

Our process and framework incorporates these concepts in this book.

Successful growth strategists are clearly not dreamers. They recognize the challenge of implementation and are able to harness the knowledge and experience in an organization to mitigate risk. In fact, successful growth strategists are risk mitigators, not risk takers. They are pragmatic and know that successful growth is measured not by what you promise, but by what you deliver. And delivery is extremely easy to measure for most clients by answering a single question: Did you hit the top line revenues associated with the plan when you were supposed to?

If it were just about sales, this would be a relatively easy exercise, but sustainable growth has to also be about return on investment (ROI) and profitability. If I gave you an unlimited budget, then inorganic growth, or growth through acquisition, would let you easily hit any revenue target. You would just buy companies until their combined revenue hit the goal you had. Problem solved, right?

While for some companies acquisition is a core weapon in their arsenal, generally the mixed bag of acquired company profitability and the ongoing challenges of integration of the different companies would likely fail on sustainability and ROI. A reality of business, especially large enterprise, is the sensitivity to a predictable, defined return on investment, so we will consider that in our process. Cost matters, and as you think about a successful growth plan, it has to include the level of expenditure required to achieve that growth.

Simply put, growth strategy is a plan to drive revenue growth. More practically, it's a way that leaders of businesses think about how they will align resourcing with opportunity to achieve a goal. As an optimist coming through the ranks in the consulting industry, I've always believed that there is no growth goal that is unachievable if the will is there. History shows that to be true, but it's never without extraordinary challenge. For sustainable success there is always a balancing act that you find best represented in the profit equation:

$$[Profit = Revenue - Cost]$$

You will always hear the critique from reviewers that a plan is "pie in the sky." By that, they really mean that the resourcing to achieve the plan isn't reasonable, or available, or within plan. We will come back to the cost side later, but what's important to realize is that cost cutting is a finite game. You can only cut cost to what is required to produce the good or service being offered. Revenue, however, is infinite, limited only by imagination and determination.

That's how you think about it, right? Entrepreneurs understand this well, as do newly minted general managers (GMs) or even those like Harrison, tasked with taking point on an annual plan. You can literally do anything to drive growth! It's overwhelming. Hell, everyone today wants to be visionary, a disruptor, a magical leader of change in the markets. Consistent growth strategy development takes time, focus, effort, and knowledge.

No one exemplifies these qualities better than James Klein, one of the most successful, accomplished strategists I know. James is the President of both the Infrastructure and Defense Products Division at

Qorvo corporation, as well as their newly formed Qorvo Biotechnolo- gies division. I can't show you his financial performance in the decades I've known him due to disclosure restrictions, but if he was a major league ball player, he'd be in the hall of fame. James has created more value for his employers in his career than just about anyone I know, but he doesn't forget how he got there.

> I grew up in technology as an engineer early on and then really went into project management and program management. And then I took over a group. So now I had a "business" to run. This was the first time I had to think – "Okay, well, I've got this thing, now what in the world do I do with it? Where do we go? Where do we invest money? What business do we want to be in?" It may have come naturally to me because of my dad. He had retired from the Air Force and started his own couple of small companies and I remember what we would usually argue about was where we should invest money. So strategy was an early thing to me. Since maybe in my teens I've thought about how you grow a business and so it's been a part of me for a long time, but probably reduced to practice when I first took over as a director of an organization.

James is a master of growth strategy development and execution. He's pretty rare. You come across people who can think about how you could grow, but very few of them are capable of driving that growth. I really enjoy his recollection of where he started:

> Early on... I was at TI (Texas Instruments) and I took over the space business. We were trying to decide what we had. We had started the space business on one very particular set of products, and we said, "now that we've got this, how do we expand it? Where else do we go?" So the first thing for me was just try to look at, what did the market look like, and it is particularly hard on the defense side to understand markets. What are we good at? What were the markets? How big could we be? What did we need to invest? And we went through that process. Now you know at TI and other large companies that usually have some guidance, you fill out these charts and so you get a little bit of guidance on how to move forward. But I would say it was really trying to understand what the market looked like and how did that intersect our technology.

I am a really big James Klein fan. And he's representative of the people I sought out to participate in this book.

Throughout this book, I'll share stories from varied perspectives at a broad array of companies. Companies matter, because they are all very different. Companies are literally "creatures" that are organically composed of people with a shared value system. You can't say "Apple announced today..." and believe that it's only a corporate act. Any announcement has been approved by legal, and not just legal: Katherine Adams, Apple's General Counsel (at the time of writing). It was also likely approved by Luca Maestri, Apple's CFO (at the time of writing), and I'm pretty sure that Tim Cook signed off as well. Investor relations, marketing, production, and sales all had to sign off on it, and because of the announcement lives are in flux. People will be hired, companies will be bought, people will be fired. Whenever I discuss the success of a growth strategy of a large company, I like to use the 50x rule. Take the number of direct staff involved in executing a strategy and multiply than number by 50. That's how many people within the company it will take for a plan to succeed, and any one of them can potentially cause it to fail.

This book is meant to serve as your playbook to develop clean, clear, effective, pragmatic, and executable growth strategies. It's for both new and existing practitioners of our art who aspire to become scientists of the discipline. Through the use of parable, framework, and process, my goal is to educate you about the method used by some of the most successful companies in the world. This method includes organic and inorganic growth, regional and global footprints, large-scale enterprise, and entrepreneurial ventures.

The truths of growth are physical laws that we are all bound by. Ideally, you read this because you want to learn, but even if you're being forced to read this for class, you'll learn something that could create a market of billions for you someday. So, open your mind, be ready to think, and enjoy learning from some of the best and brightest business minds in the world as they tell you their story. This is incredibly fun stuff, and if you are lucky enough to be responsible for this function, then you know it's pretty rarefied air and should be savored.

1

The Growth Matrix and the Four Key Questions

Growth is an infinite game, with the revenue line limited only by your ability to convince new or existing customers to buy the products or services you currently or will produce.

Ever think about how to bound the question of growth? I'm a growth strategist, so I worry quite a bit about the sources of growth. Where does growth come from?

Turns out the question has a simple answer.

All revenues come from two variables: (1) customers and (2) the goods/services they buy. Full stop. It's really that simple: *who* buys and *what* they buy. Every business, from the first fish seller bartering his daily catch for salt to the world's biggest consumer goods company, grapples with these two fundamental questions. Let's talk about customers first.

Customers

There are all kinds of customers and they have different values to companies when considered over a time period.

Kevin Watters is blazing fast in every sense. Physically, he's a marathoner who is a top competitor for his age group. He processes information quickly and insightfully. He is quick to offer his help, and his fast-tracked career is an incredible success story. Currently retired and an adjunct professor at Tulane's Freeman School of Business, Kevin started his career in consumer packaged goods working for Proctor & Gamble, where he received his "MBA on top of an MBA" through their training program. He then went on to dip his toe in entrepreneurial waters, got married to his amazing wife, Fern, had their first child, and then he needed to go back into the corporate world. He found his way into the world of online banking in 1999 and never looked back. He joined Bank One, and was noticed by Jamie Dimon, who asked him to take over as President of their Consumer Internet Group. From there Kevin took over wholesale banking. When Bank One was acquired by JPMorgan Chase, he took over as CEO of business banking and grew it to over a billion-dollar business. Being one of the few businesses that managed credit well through the Great Recession, he was asked to fix the wreckage that was the mortgage portfolio, which he did. In his final role at JPMorgan Chase, Kevin took over as CEO of their credit card business. We talked about the true value of customers in the world of financial services.

> Banking is a little bit interesting. It doesn't matter what age you are when you go into Starbucks and you buy a latte. Whether you're 25 or 65, your latte is the same price. Well, in banking chances are if you're 65, you've got a lot more money than when you were 25. So part of the game is for your existing customers to stay with you, with the more money they have. In your 30s you're borrowing for your mortgage, in your 40s, your investment account is growing so great, let's make sure we've got your mortgage and your investment account. You know in your 20s, I want to make sure you've got a credit card and I have your checking account, but I'm getting everything else as you grow. Within your life I'm growing with you, and then I'm getting your retirement account. I'm growing up with you, which is a little bit different than other products where you know, like you're buying your latte if you're 25 or 65, is still $4 and thanks. Much different in the banking world.

I loved the insight Kevin's example gave. This is just one industry. Every industry and business has their own version of this.

As strategists, there are a few important things to consider when you think about customers that I want to talk a bit about. Some basic rules of thumb:

- All money comes from your customers.
- All customers are not equal.
- Customers buy differently.

All Money Comes from Your Customers

Sounds obvious, but unless you are a business owner, or tasked with top-line growth, it is very easy for businesses to lose sight of this simple fact. Why? Because you get wrapped up in your everyday work process, and you can't see the clear link between your customers and your paycheck. At Starbucks, it's easy to see how customers fuel the business. It's a direct transaction: A customer orders a latte, swipes a card, and gets a latte. Any employee can see how that customer relates to their paycheck.

However, in some industries there are indirect customers whom you serve. Healthcare is a great example. Depending on where you live in the world, most providers are reimbursed from either a public or private "payer" (insurance company). Money doesn't come from patients, right? Well, ultimately, Medicare, Medicaid, and military insurance programs are funded through tax dollars. In those public programs, taxes come from the country's citizens, who are, effectively, its customers. Private insurers are paid by employers or individuals, so even though it's indirect, the customer still pays the bills. These are extreme examples, but you get the point.

We also have many clients who worry about their customer's customer. That is, let's say you manufacture a radio component that is part of the Tesla system. You aren't really designing functionality for Tesla; you are designing for Tesla owners (the end users) or your customer's customer. So even though your bills are paid by Tesla, without Tesla's customer base you won't get paid for very long. That means you likely work to understand the end user's wants and needs. As we consider

11

... revenue – our customers – we have to be sensitive to ...ect trail that the money may flow through.

All Customers Are Not Equal

Every business has preferred customers. Starbucks has their regu-lar early morning work crowd, and they also happen to serve any out-of-town tourists who strolled in that day. Amazon has major named accounts that spend billions with their Amazon Web Services (AWS) business, and they have Cliff Farrah, who spends a whole bunch during the holidays, but is otherwise pretty much a non-event to their business. All customers are not equal. As a strategist it's important to understand and grow the best sources of our revenue and make sure we are focused on them.

Customers Buy Differently

Not every customer acquires in the same way. Some pay cash, others use credit. Some want to own, some want to rent. Some pay by the month, some pay by the drink. As strategists, we have to make it easy for all our different customers to provide us with revenue.

Now let's shift to the second question: What do the customers buy?

Goods and Services

If all money flows from customers, what they buy is driven by the goods and services that you offer. There are some great books about how to market and sell goods and services, and the experts we've interviewed throughout this book will give you real insight into best practices to maximize growth, but before we go swim in the deep end, I'd like to make sure we are aligned on some basic thoughts about goods and services and why they are procured.

- Some goods and services fill a market need; many fill a want.
- Goods and services are definable, measurable offerings.
- They are things that can be valued.

Some Goods and Services Fill a Market Need: Many Fill a Want

As a formally trained economist, I still think in terms of utility and supply and demand. These principles are based on having something of
value that is sought in the market. There are lots of ways that products
are created, and we talk about a number of examples later in the book,
but at the end of the day, we buy things that we need (food, water,
shelter, clothing), and things that we want, but don't really need. Sometimes it's a want that is strong enough to make them frivolously spend
money. Let's face it, the latest AirPods Pro aren't a need, but nutri-
tious food is. We don't have to have ice cream cones, but we do need
clean water. Wants have very different challenges in driving growth than
needs. Realize what you are offering as you consider how to grow.

Goods and Services Are Definable, Measurable Offerings

In order to transact, you have to be able to bound your offering. People
need to know what they are getting for what they are paying. In some
markets this is pretty straightforward. You go to a shoe store and buy a
pair of shoes. Definable/measurable. When you get into services, things
get much harder to bound. Toss in "as a service" and you'll find that
lawyers are making a lot of money bounding definitions of what you are
and are not buying, as well as your rights to any data produced by your
usage. Understanding what you are selling, especially as companies
move to offerings that marry product, service, and software, is really
important.

I talked about this a bit with my good friend Ray Ausrotas. Ray is
one of Boston's successful trial attorneys, a twice-published author of
Lexis practice guides, and has helped me several times throughout
the years as Beacon has protected much of its own proprietary and
confidential information. He is smart, tireless, fierce, and yet kind and
reasonable. Killer combination. I cannot recommend him highly enough
should you ever need a litigator. We talked about how poorly written
and defined services agreements can lead to bad outcomes:

> Especially in the services world, communication and clarity defining the
> scope of what is going to be a continuing business relationship – where
> both sides understand precisely what is being delivered, and how and
> when – is critical. If parties structuring their interactions rush this process

(or get "go fever") at the outset, or don't adjust when circumstances have changed, it is not unusual to see litigation occur. Many of the commercial cases I have litigated and tried over the last 20-plus years have had poorly defined terms at their core. Of course parties can't realistically expect to foresee and negotiate risks for every future situation they will encounter; but hard work on the front end, with each side specifying and adequately protecting their rights (including over who holds rights to proprietary business confidential information and intellectual property), can help to prevent costly and unpredictable outcomes down the road.

He's right. In the services world, or in the product world, what you sell needs to be clearly understood and defined. There are too many snakes out there who are all too willing to bite.

They Are Things That Can Be Valued

It may sound obvious, but in my world, growth often comes from new ideas that create goods and services that don't yet exist. We work to help our clients "value," or assign a dollar amount to, their idea. Later on we'll talk about how different companies approach this, but if you want to sell something, the market has to perceive value in it. No matter how cool a new product is, or how much time you've invested in it, there has to be a perceived value proposition that is well understood by the client.

Combine these two most important factors and you create the revenue matrix.

The Revenue Matrix

When customers and goods/services collide, four sources of growth result:

1. An existing client and an existing product
2. An existing client and a new product/service
3. A new client and a new product/service
4. A new client and an existing product/service

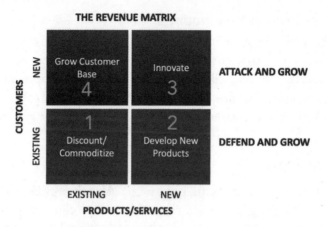

FIGURE 1.1 The Revenue Matrix

If you put them together in a two-by-two table, you get the Revenue Matrix that presents these categories visually (Figure 1.1).

This is an extremely powerful way to think about the sources of revenue, and you can easily use this matrix to segment your current portfolio and growth plan. I've used this matrix throughout my career to consider how to drive revenue.

Defend and Grow

The first two quadrants deal with "Defend and Grow" opportunities, which are driven by existing client relationships. You want to defend them against competitors, but also grow what they spend with you over time.

Quadrant 1: Discount/Commoditize

Selling *existing* customers *existing* products and services is a staple for a sustainable business. This is where I would expect to see the vast majority of revenues come from in a business older than 1 year. Over time, in most businesses, this bucket declines due to commoditization. You get stale. You are vulnerable to a competitor's fresher, more interesting offering.

Quadrant 2: Develop New Products

Next is the lower right-hand quadrant, or selling *existing* customers *new* products and services. By developing or offering new products and services to existing clients, you leverage the goodwill you have already generated and are able to counter commoditization and price erosion in the prior quadrant.

Attack and Grow

The next two "top" quadrants deal with "Attack and Grow" opportunities. These are where you are acquiring a new client, typically taking them away from another vendor. Typically a heavier lift and riskier effort.

Quadrant 3: Innovate

Acquiring *new* customers and *new* product revenues, or the upper right-hand quadrant of the matrix, is a "share grab". . . using a new product to take away customers from competitors. This is an expected and classic strategy in the game of product improvement. You can see that across industries – the launch of a new phone, the introduction of a new COVID antibody test, the development of a new shoe fashion – each of these can attract new customers because they want a new product.

Quadrant 4: Grow Customer Base

New customers buying *existing* products and services has a variety of causes typically associated with its selection, including the failure of a competitor's product (supply chain or product dissatisfaction) or strategies of bundling with newer more disruptive products to allow access. Often times it follows an increase in sales focus on a new customer community or geography.

Oliver Richards has been a part of Beacon's story for the past decade. Senior Vice President and leader of our Healthcare and Lifesciences practice, Oliver is also my chief growth officer and is fundamental in driving the success of our firm. A University of Chicago undergrad in chemistry followed up by a PhD in cellular and molecular biology and an MBA from Wisconsin, Oliver is not only brilliant, he's also a great husband and father, and takes care of all teammates and clients in his orbit. We talked a bit about the four quadrants of the Revenue Matrix.

> I think by nature what we do is look at the new and the unknown quite a bit. And so I think we spend probably a disproportionate amount of time on new products and new customers. Probably in the existing customer, new product, new customer, existing product. We focus there versus where our clients spend the bulk of their time, in the existing customer, existing product bucket.

He's right; we do tend to work on the emerging end of things at Beacon, and Oliver helps his clients drive significant growth in these vectors. As consultants, we love two-by-two matrices. They are easy to write, easy to understand, and if they work, they are generally powerful; if they don't, you toss them out! Like all frameworks, they give structure to challenges and problems, which is one of the goals of this book. However, we have additional goals beyond structuring the problem. We want our output to be pragmatic, actionable, and exhaustive in the planning process. A two-by-two illustration alone doesn't achieve that.

The Four Key Questions: Customers

Growth strategy is complex. Growth strategy is risky. Growth strategy is an art that can't be taught. These are three of the biggest myths in enterprise business today. If you can answer four questions for your business, you can develop a growth strategy. The questions are simple, powerful, and linked to both risk and reward.

When I started Beacon, the challenge I had was to teach my way of thinking to the people I worked with. There is quite a bit of subjectivity to the approach, but over time I was able to determine that there were objective key risk/reward questions that drove success and failure as my clients executed growth plans in their worlds.

Beyond customer and goods/services elements, there is a near-limitless group of questions that strategists consider depending on their industry and company. It's what I call the Strategist's Challenge: If there are no boundaries to your creativity, how do you know what to focus on?

I always have looked at decision-making from a pareto position. What are the most critical things to worry about as you plan a successful growth strategy? The initial, most clarifying questions to help a strategist plan and focus? The greatest risk/reward variables? Based on my analysis and experience, there are Four Key Questions to consider.

- Which CUSTOMERS will I serve?
- Which GEOGRAPHIES AND LOCATIONS will I serve?
- What GOODS AND SERVICES will I sell?
- What BUSINESS MODEL will I use?

Our work shows that if you can answer these questions, you can build a successful growth strategy. If you miss on these, it's pretty tough to do well.

Our next chapter focuses on Question 1: Which customers will I serve?

CHAPTER

2

Which CUSTOMERS Will I Serve?

We talked about the value of a customer as the source of all revenue in Chapter 1. What we didn't talk about is how important choosing wisely is. **Whom you choose to sell to is the single most critical question a company must answer.** The amount of time and energy that goes into customer acquisition is staggering, and for good reason. It is a much more efficient, less risky proposition to sell to an existing customer than it is to sell to a new customer. But new customers are generally aligned with growth for a new business. What percentage of your time and energy should be focused on existing versus new customers?

As you ponder this, let's make it real. There are only 24 hours in a day. There are only so many employees you can lean on. There are only so many dollars you can spend. As an entrepreneur, this is an intuitive set of data. Your gut tells you what you can and cannot support. At a larger enterprise, it's a more formal budgeting process. But in either model, you need to think about where to focus your limited resources.

Older companies tend to have more customers to serve, and care and feeding of those customers becomes the primary objective of the revenue engine. David Maister, former Harvard Business School professor, consultant, and best selling author, coined the phrase, "hunters and farmers." Older companies, with more mature processes and client relationships tend to "farm," meaning they rely on existing customers, while younger companies or product lines tend to "hunt," or look for new customers. From a skills standpoint, it's generally accepted that it's easier to find and develop farmers than hunters, and that is simply because you can rely on the legacy of the relationship and brand that has been developed over time as a farmer.

We will talk more about this in later chapters, but without a doubt, the customers you choose to serve are the critical first growth question to consider.

How your revenue breaks down has a lot to do with what kind of company you work for. As a start-up, you will find much of your effort focused on the addition of new customers, where a more mature business focuses more on generating more from existing customers. The revenue mix changes over time as customers become repeat businesses.

Doug Fletcher is the modern-day version of a Renaissance man. An author, professor, board member, speaker, consultant, and former member of GE's management development program – I've known and respected Doug's contributions to business thought since we sat next to each other over 25 years ago at the Darden Graduate School of Business at UVA. He's a proud dad, a killer fly fisherman, and one of the most pragmatic people I know. I was lucky enough to corral Doug into offering up some of his wisdom in this book. Doug is a specialist in the world of services in general and professional services in particular. He teaches consultants, accountants, lawyers, engineers, system integrators, and financial service practitioners how to attract new customers. If you are lucky enough to have a chance to sit in on one of his sessions, I highly recommend it. Doug has two great books under his belt, his first as a coauthor and the latest solo. It's called *How to Win Client Business* and talks about the challenges of getting new clients.

This is generally accepted as the single hardest act in services business development, and we talked a bit about why:

> We need our existing customers most in the world that I come from. In professional services your existing client base is probably 70% to 80% plus of your revenue stream, and yet if we don't have that 20% of new client growth, ultimately, businesses will plateau or decline because of churn with the existing client base. So we need new clients.

Doug is spot on with this assessment in our world and truly for most businesses. All money comes from customers. New customers are the hardest thing to add, and they represent growth. Doug went on to describe other value new clients provide:

> From a cultural and organizational behavior perspective, you need that new client base to create excitement and growth opportunities for your people! If your business is growing, you're going to have opportunities for everyone. So from a behavioral and a financial standpoint, I think new client growth is important and I have spent my focus over the last 5 years for both of these books on how to win new client business. And I made it very clear in my new book that it's not that the existing clients are not important. They are vitally important! It's just that what most people get hung up on is "How do I get new clients?" It goes back to Maister's "hunter" versus "farmer" thing, and I think while there are a lot of really good farmers out there, finding good hunters is hard.

Whenever Doug offers his wisdom, I always find myself reflecting on it a day or two after the conversation. If you didn't get the nuance of his discussion, I'd encourage you to take your time and perhaps read it through twice . . . slowly.

Customers, customers, customers . . . which customers will I serve? Will they be direct or indirect? How do I define a customer? To appreciate the variety of viewpoints on what a customer is, I cast a wide net in my interviews and included a variety of industry leaders. Here's the perspective of a man who humbles me.

Mitch Mongell and I became friends about 6 or 7 years ago through a shared love of golf. A fierce competitor, Mitch participated in and was a generous supporter of an event I created called the NAA, a fundraiser for the Crohn's and Colitis Foundation of America. Mitch is the CEO of the Fort Walton Beach Medical Center in Florida, a division of HCA Healthcare, one of the leading US healthcare providers with more than 180 hospitals and 2,000 sites of care in the US and UK markets. They earned over $51 billion in 2019. As I researched the company, I was impressed to read that the CEO was returning $6 billion in CARES Act funding because the company leadership felt despite being legally eligible, it was the right thing to do.

Mitch has been with HCA since 1996 in a variety of roles. Prior to joining HCA, he worked for the Cleveland Clinic, and is a Fellow in the American College of Healthcare Executives. He has an MBA from Florida Atlantic University and served as a registered nurse and paramedic/EMT. He has walked on both sides of the track in healthcare and has an empathy for his patients and his team that I truly admire. He looks at customers in a way that I don't. His way is incredibly valid and, to me, oddly comforting.

> Well, it's interesting as you look at customers, who are our customers. That's probably one of the most difficult questions that you have. Our customers can be our community where the hospital is. The customers are also the physicians who[m] you try to attract and who provide great service. The patients you serve. And many times, the patient's family become a customer. The payer sources, whether it be Medicare or Medicaid, the VA, private insurance, or those that have self-pay, whether it's cash or whether it's charity care. We have those different types of customers we serve.

As a firm, currently our largest practice area is focused on healthcare, and as you can imagine, I think it is one of the most meaningful areas we add value. When you look at the question of customer through the lens that Mitch uses, it's quite a different perspective.

> Each hospital tends to be a little bit different. Our hospital serves an existing base that has been here for years. The community of Fort Walton/Destin has an image set in their mind of who we were maybe 10–12 years ago. For community hospitals, bigger was always better for higher-level care. We have worked to rebrand so we teach existing customers we can provide that service better here. One: We know you. Two: You don't have to travel . . . we bring the qualified physicians here, whether it be from Mayo Clinic, Cleveland Clinic, etc.

The new customers will be those who are vacationing. The 260,000 people we have in our community swells to a million any given day during Memorial Day and Labor Day and then December 15th through March 15th we have all the snowbirds who come down, so different types of payer sources and different types of customers altogether.

We talked about the unusual impact of natural events in his world relating to how he gets and serves new customers. In particular, we discussed 2018's Hurricane Michael that decimated nearby Panama City, Florida.

Well, that's what's great about our company HCA. We work together as teams. We saw the hurricane coming, and all of ACA prepares like we are the third little pig, with the nice brick house. We were prepared for the storm but it turned east and our sister hospital down in Panama City was severely impacted. (Author's note: 2 years later the city is still rebuilding.) We put together a helicopter landing service here. We just took over a doctor's office parking lot and made more availability for helicopters to fly patients in from those hospitals that were hit. What a disruption not only from the ER standpoint, surgery standpoint, skilled nursing facilities, assisted living facilities. It was just extremely impactful. Then moving the children so they could come back to school. We even set up networks in order to get these patients in touch with their families and also to be cared for and then housed temporarily until we could find safe haven for them to go back to.
We were receiving 30 flights a day.

I share Mitch's story to illustrate just how many ways you can define *customer:* direct, indirect, community, colleague. Sometimes you have to think about the ecosystem you serve in its entirety. Oftentimes, neglect of one segment of your customer base will impact another. Mitch is not just addressing his customer base, but the ecosystem created within the hospital itself and how all the parts need to function together to address his customer's needs. Only focusing on the patients and neglecting the community would not ultimately benefit his company as a whole.

He's right about the constituencies he needs to serve, but we still need to focus on who buys our goods and services, and I think by and large that all businesses do.

The bottom line on customers is well understood. Assuming you have a good relationship with a customer, it is almost always easier and more profitable to sell to an existing customer than to acquire a new customer. In acquiring a new customer, you have to create awareness that you exist, interest in learning about your product/service, and desire to try it out. With an existing customer, that is all sunk cost and should be a much more efficient exercise. Existing customers are also more likely to buy again and again, and in some industries can be understood as an annuity. Acquiring new customers is generally a harder, much costlier, and higher-risk proposition.

3

Which GEOGRAPHIES AND LOCATIONS Will I Serve?

One of the highest risk variables to consider is the notion of geographic expansion.

When you think about expanding to a new physical infrastructure, you amass financial, logistical, and managerial risk. This is true whether you are thinking about opening a new venue in the next town or you are thinking about entering another country. The further the distance, the greater the risk.

Companies pursue geographic growth in a variety of ways, but they boil down mostly to organic and inorganic activity. Organic would be build. Inorganic would be buy. Build-versus-buy is generally accepted as a critical decision when considering growth options, and it's particularly true when you think about the geographies you will serve.

When you pursue geographic growth, you run straight into a number of risks:

- Build cost
- Regulatory/taxation requirements
- Offset requirements
- Repatriation challenges
- Recruiting talent
- Acquisition costs (inorganic)
- Distribution ecosystem
- Customer acquisition cost

But, like most things that involve risk, there is also reward. By growing geographically you get

- Access to entirely new customer base
- Diversification of economic risk
- Potential for growth at multiple levels
- Test bed for new business models
- New ideas that can be applied to existing geos

Older, larger companies that have worked through geographic expansion have a tremendous advantage in their ongoing operations that align with these benefits.

There are some really interesting stories out there about epic fails on geographic expansion. Take your pick . . . Target's withdrawal from Canada after two years and billions of dollars spent. Home Depot's 2006–2012 failed foray into China. Walmart's 1997 failed launch of 85 stores in Germany. Starbucks' 14-year misstep in Australia. Best Buy's 2010/2011 failed attempt to grow in the UK. And these misses had massive economic impact on their parent companies, not to mention the damage to brand around the globe.

Does this question hold in a post-COVID world? The notion of a large-scale company with an entirely remote workforce changing the dynamic of this risk after the pandemic isn't so far-fetched. Several leading companies have announced plans to either entirely or partially have remote staff, with Alphabet, Google's parent company, considering a hybrid policy of three days in, two days out at the time of writing.[1] There is precedent to refer to as you think about this future state. IBM began experimenting with this in 1979, and in 2009 reported over 40% of its workforce had no physical office.[2] The game changed in 2017, when IBM started to force thousands of workers back into the office. The link between an office setting and productivity concerns had them reverse their position. The notion of work-from-home isn't new. Gallup estimated in 2017 that 43% of workers in the US were remote! The data shows that through these periods, companies continued to expand their geographic footprint, and while during the time of pandemic a number of us are required to be remote, we will continue to see office presence as a key component of collaboration and growth. Assuming there is no health reason to prevent us from working together, as humans we will continue to seek the office environment and in-person client interactions as the continuing standard for productivity and sustainable growth. That's why even in a post-COVID world, despite the likely increase in hybrid workforce, this key question stands.

The statistics are remarkable as you consider the investment required to support international growth. In a 2015 *Harvard Business Review* piece, Christian Stadler, Michael Mayer, and Julia Hautz estimate that it takes 10 years to generate a 1% return on assets from global expansion! They studied 20,000 companies in 30 countries that attempted this.[3] Wow.

However, I didn't title this question "which country" – I chose "which geography." By that I mean simple physical geographic expansion, typically to access a new set of customers. Clearly global or international expansion falls under this umbrella, but so do less glamorous expansions.

A restaurant is a great way to illustrate the levels of choice open to companies considering geographic expansion today. A US business could expand locally (next town over), intrastate, interstate, or internationally. The risk goes up each step of the way. Let's say you own the best steakhouse in Dallas. With your partner, you've decided that you want to add a new location (aka geography) to drive growth. Where do you locate? If you stay within a 30-minute drive, you get the benefit of people knowing your brand and the option for existing staff to support new operations. Great! But you'll run out of customers pretty quickly, so what about a new spot in Houston? Still in Texas, so you know your state tax code and requirements, but you can't leverage your staff, and your brand may not be as good. Let's say Houston is a hit, and now you decide to be bold and try a move to Atlanta. Suddenly you have to worry about the logistics of remote management, the creation of brand, supplier, employee, and the development of a new customer base. Throw on top of that the added cost of airfare for senior management to run back and forth, the tax ramifications of nexus in another state (may want to look that one up if you don't know), and the hurdles to clear become much higher. Of course, all new customers and a growing brand, diversification of revenues, and a wonderful marketing tale for your other stores are the potential offset, but the risk factors go up. Clearly the more remote the location, the greater the risk of quality control issues or the dilution of your original vision.

Let's take it up a notch. What about opening up your next steakhouse in Paris, London, Beijing, or Moscow? Now you have international tax code to become expert in. You also need to meet new legal standards for employees, food production, an entirely new marketing spend. The logistics of management now not only span distance but also time zones, language, and cultural barriers. This is incredibly expensive and risky . . . especially for a restaurant.

But what about other industries?

I had a chance to interview long time client and strategy guru John Beering. I've worked with John during his time at Pratt & Whitney (where he served as the Director of Marketing for Commercial Engines and Global Service Providers), Eaton Corporation (as Senior Vice President and General Manager of their Commercial Powertrain business), Trojan Battery Company (serving as Chief Operating Officer), and caught up with him in his new role as President and Board Member of United Access and Arch Channel Retail, the second largest retailer of wheelchair-accessible vans in the US.

John had been responsible for global expansion in a number of his roles, and I asked him about the realities for industrial corporations considering that kind of move. He reflected on his time at Eaton, serving large automotive and trucking OEM partners like Daimler, Mercedes-Benz, Volkswagen Group, and Volvo:

> I think when we were looking at trying to do a major expansion, China or India would be a good example, you really had to think through method of entry. We're going to go look at an acquisition? Is a joint venture going to be more appropriate? Is export even viable? If [the answer is] yes to any of those [questions], what is that going to look like? For a JV, what's the endgame? Can you do it in a way that's successful? Our preference at the time was majority ownership for joint ventures. Being majority owners allowed us to roll it up and report the earnings. It also meant that we had control over the operating approach. You know, prior to my time there they had some JVs in the same geographies that didn't go so well. In hindsight, the prior Chinese JVs were either 50/50 or the Chinese partner had the control and so of course they played by different rules. Eaton also made the mistake previously of having a different deal team from the integration and management teams. This meant they lost relationship continuity – which is everything in China. Eaton also maintained a strong culture centered on doing business right – their ethical North Star. Operating in China (or many Asian countries for that matter), where the local leadership's worldview and business standards and practices are just different than ours. Assuming they will automatically adjust to our Western standards was naïve and unrealistic. This is why the relationships are so important. You need the relationship foundation to establish trust and work through misunderstandings over time. Where we had established bases of operations in China or India, then the challenge centered [on] how to partner more meaningfully with key customers. They might say, "Let's do a joint venture . . . and we want the joint venture on site. We probably wanted it on our existing campus to capitalize on our existing investments. The next requirement was if we were going to have a volume commitment from the customer partner to make this business venture work. And then if we take product in the other markets, are we protected on IP and things like that? Among the biggest items in the foreign JVs is protecting IP [intellectual property] and being mindful not to enable a new competitor unintentionally in other established markets. Other important considerations include talent availability, capital and operating costs, tax structure and cash repatriation, currency risk, etc.

Geographic expansion in the corporate world is high-stakes poker, and that makes this question the number-two concern on the list to consider.

However, larger businesses of scale have a *tremendous* advantage leveraging their existing geographic footprint. If you've already worked through the hurdles that John raised, then that is a huge competitive advantage. Doug Fletcher talked a bit more about this very point:

> It's so much easier to hunt in an existing geography for professional services than it is in a new geography. And maybe it's true with products, too, but it's especially true in a service business because services are such relationship sales and people naturally trust people [who] are from their area more than people from faraway places. Example: If I'm from New York and I want to sell in Mobile, Alabama, that's going to be a hard sell, right? But if you're in New York and you're trying to expand into Connecticut or New Jersey, that's an easier sale. New geography is hard in the services business because you have no established brand reputation and you have no established relationship base; you're looking at a multiyear proposition before you can expect any sort of traction.

Michael Woodfolk, President of the Darden School Foundation, and I spoke a bit about their recent expansion to the DC Metro area. Michael is smart, effective, kind, and polished. He's the friend you wish you had more of in your life. Michael has an incredibly challenging role as the head of a 501(c)(3) that is the funding engine of UVA's Darden School. He's led this organization for the past 5 years, although he's been at the school for over 20 and is a fellow graduate. He illustrated how through its recent geographic expansion the school has been able to drive growth, not just by accessing new students, but by better engagement with alumni:

> We had to innovate. Our innovation was to launch the executive MBA at our new UVA Darden Sands Family Grounds, our DC Metro facility in Washington, which is very different than Charlottesville, Virginia, . . . We launched an executive MBA there and since our largest alumni base sits within Washington, DC, all of a sudden Darden becomes more real to alumni. You're all busy, we just have to make sure we figure out a way to be relevant to you and part of being relevant is being seen. That big sign that used to say USA TODAY on a huge building in Arlington, VA, now says UVA Darden School . . . so it's not just Charlottesville anymore. It's now Washington, DC. It's not just the traditional MBA, it's the executive, and we're already thinking about, what's next? The night MBA? We have the marketplace to do that now.

Michael showed a success story for expansion, but as a rule, existing geographies are the low-risk route. Site location, build-out cost, staffing challenges, maintenance, and operations can be significant unknowns. More concerning is the potential for the geography's ability to sustain the revenues necessary for the investment to access that market physically. New geographies offer access to new customer pools, and a non-core test environment for new products/business model testing.

Notes

1. Charlie Osborne, "Google Slams on the Brakes for Office Return, Mulls 'Flexible Work Week,'" ZD Net, December 14, 2020, https://www .zdnet.com/article/google-slams-on-the-brakes-for-office-return-mulls-flexible-work-week/.
2. Jerry Useem, "When Working from Home Doesn't Work," The Atlantic, November 2017, https://www.theatlantic.com/magazine/archive/2017/ 11/when-working-from-home-doesnt-work/540660/.
3. Christian Stadler, Michael Mayer, and Julia Hautz, "Few Companies Actually Succeed at Going Global," Harvard Business Review, June 2015, https://hbr.org/2015/03/few-companies-actually-succeed-at-going-global.

4

What GOODS AND SERVICES Will I Sell?

Third on our list is what you sell. Goods and services are things a company sells to generate revenue. It is a truth that without a client there is no revenue, but it's also true that without the right goods and services, there is no revenue, either. You can't gloss over this.

It is incredibly hard to know what the right goods and services are. Generally, there are two approaches that bound how most companies approach product development: You can either study the market for unmet needs or whitespace opportunities, or you can create markets with new product and service concepts that haven't been seen before. Both are hard to do well, typically require a significant amount of time and investment, and often fail.

Corning has been producing innovative products for 169 years at the time of writing. I've been lucky enough to work with Corning for a number of years, and one of my favorite people there is Corning's Innovation Officer, Marty Curran. Marty embodies the kind of client that you

hope to get a chance to work with. He's smart, funny, thoughtful, pragmatic, and, ultimately, a great leader. I first worked with Marty when he
was the general manager of Corning Cable Systems, and in 2004/2005
we worked deploying a little thing called fiber to the home with Verizon
Fios (acronym for Fiber Optic Service), which was the first major deployment of bundled video, phone, and data high-speed access. While it's a
proven technology now, back then it was a big risk, and like all product
development, timing is everything.

> Typical in Corning . . . Many times when the invention is made it is a little
> bit too early . . . can be as much as 15 years too early. People will say,
> you guys are "patient money" – and the answer is, we are not! Every
> year the budget comes up and there's a constant discussion whether
> you stop doing something . . . [often] you will shelve the technology
> . . . Then, a customer will have a problem, and you'll go back, find that
> technology – and use it. That's what happened with Gorilla Glass.

For those of you who don't know what I'm talking about, there's the
famous story of Gorilla Glass, the glass substrate that Corning provided
to Apple after Steve Jobs discovered that the plastic screen originally
designed for the iPhone scratched easily. The inside baseball story is
that while Corning typically could take 1 to 3 years to create a new
product, Jobs needed it in under 6 months. Corning did what they do
really well, which is to look to use technology from the past that might
fit the bill – and found something built decades earlier for automotive
glass that never took hold (in this case, it was too good!).

> It was the idea of having an incredibly strong auto glass and it went into
> hibernation for a little while. Our chairman always loved the technology,
> the idea of making glass stronger. His stretch goal for our technical orga-
> nization: "Can you make a glass that cannot be broken?" And he trotted
> [it] back out and when he met with Steve Jobs for a completely different
> reason . . . we climbed on . . . this older technology and with changes,
> turned it into something brand new.

Now, for every Gorilla Glass and fiber optic example at Corning,
there are many more programs and projects that haven't succeeded
(and may be needed years if not decades later). In fact, we now take

fiber optics for granted, but according to Marty, it took 4 years for optical fiber to be taken from a theory invented by a Nobel Prize winner to a product that worked by Corning scientists. That same optical fiber innovation powers the internet today. So, the timing of product development and introduction is everything. What's really important to understand about Corning is that they are really good at growing their top line.

> There was a calculation done by our finance folks, seems in the last 20 years we [Corning] made more money than in the first 150 combined . . . I give a lot of that credit to our chairman who created a strategy and growth framework. We're going to lean into growing and innovating and at the same time we're going to spend a lot of time on execution. In the old days Corning would invent something. Then they would sell the business when it hit maturity and reinvest into another invention. We realized that we could excel in operations, manage the business from cradle to grave, capturing the cash flow from an aging business, and reinvesting that cash into the next business and our shareholders.

Marty shared a COVID example of how market demand and independent lab research have recently collided for Corning.

> We've got a fabulous little technology now – Guardiant – that is a combination of copper and glass ceramic. You can imbed this invention into materials. For instance, we can sprinkle this "pixie dust" into paint. When mixed, you have an anti-viral, antimicrobial paint that can kill 99.9% of bad germs in under two hours. Interesting time for an interesting invention.

So, will Guardiant be another hit? Hard to say, but Marty Curran will always make sure Corning has a rich mixture of technology and market- and demand-driven goods and services available for his clients.

One last area I think is critical to consider when developing new products is the challenge and likelihood of failure. Culturally, it's very difficult for most companies to embrace failure. No one likes to fail, and it's costly to embrace this as a part of your business. In tech-heavy companies like Corning, engineers can dedicate years of their lives to projects that may never achieve market success. Learning to value the effort, acknowledge the learnings, and to celebrate those who failed is a counterintuitive cultural strength that only a few companies have.

Marty: We have a project every Halloween . . . and we have people get up for the projects we killed in the past year to get on stage to say "What were you trying to do?" "What did you learn?" and "Whom do we thank?" Because we were told by people that whenever we shelved projects, people weren't getting recognized. We decided that maybe we ought to talk about those things a little more, so we have a little recognition now to help us learn why did this thing fail?

Cliff: So the value in this process is seen in the Gorilla Glass example. You guys developed it 25 years earlier.

Marty: Research kept it in their library.

Cliff: And then you brought it to market. Six months to production.

Marty: Building on that base technology, creating an updated product. Yes.

Corning is the real deal. They are seeing growth due to their excellence and discipline in developing, offering, archiving, and stockpiling new capabilities. A practitioner can learn quite a bit from how Corning is shepherding their innovation culture and decision-making process.

I introduced you last chapter to John Beering from United Access, and he offered an independent confirmation of Corning's approach from his days at Eaton Corporation.

It's important to understand, especially [for] innovations, that sometimes you're going to fail and it's really important to embrace failure as a learning opportunity and to do some sort of diagnostic on it. Doesn't have to be super-sophisticated, but an inspection of what happened. What was the root cause [of failure]? If we're going to try it again, what are we going to do differently? I had a conversation today with one of my regional VPs who said, "Well, you know, we've tried that before and it didn't work . . ." I said, "Yes, but this set of variables is different now, so it might work this time. Or how might it be different?" We have to turn that thinking around so that we don't bury all the skeletons; we actually look at the corpses and do autopsy and learn from them and then try it again.

It is also important to draw a distinction between *goods* and *services*. In order for the model and process we present in this book to work across every form of business we needed to consider both manufacturing and services economies. In fact at our firm, most clients offer both to the market.

In life, if you are lucky, you meet and learn from accomplished people. When I was cutting my teeth after business school, I met Don Scales after he learned of my apprenticeship with David Maister. Don is a friend and mentor who has served on Beacon's board of directors for many years. A graduate of Rice University with a master's degree in chemical engineering, Don followed this with an MBA at Harvard. In the services world, Don is an iconic figure who has led some of the largest professional services practices in the world. Formerly the head of Arthur D. Little's Aerospace and Defense practice, he led AT Kearney's Industry Verticals after their acquisition by EDS. He then moved to Oracle led all of the Industry Vertical consulting for Oracle, reporting to Larry Ellison. At that point Don saw the writing on the wall and pivoted to enabling the digital economy as CEO of iCrossing (which was successfully acquired by Hearst Corporation), and currently serves as the CEO of Investis Digital, a leader in the digital marketing domain. Don is also the author of two books, and splits his time between Manhattan and London. We spent some time talking about the productization of services.

> When I started, there was no such thing as having a services business be part of a software company. Those two were still separate and then you saw people like Oracle and other software companies try to start getting into the services business when they found out there was lots of money to be made in services and implementation. I think in some ways that started the ball rolling toward where we are today.
> When Oracle started a services business, they looked at services as a loss leader that was going to "open the door." If we give away enough services, they'll buy more software. As the head of a consulting firm, I didn't get into business to be a loss leader, so I had to drive cultural change, and there was a big conflict for a number of years at places like Oracle until they figured out that they can make as much or more money on services than they could on software. Then it got to a place where it was sort of a marriage, because then they were equal partners . . . You have to realize that you may or may not like services, but you can make a lot of money at it if you do it right.

In my career, I've worked with a number of clients who were trying to figure out how to monetize services dollars. We didn't always call it "monetization" – that is a relatively new term – but we thought a lot about it because it was a new revenue stream in the market that was emerging from traditional services providers. Gartner defines a system integrator as "an enterprise that specializes in implementing, planning, coordinating, scheduling, testing, improving, and sometimes maintaining a computing operation" on their website. As you think about this, know that every function listed has been around for quite a long time. But historically it was a giveaway. Now it's sold separately as a service. I've worked through this process at dozens of companies that have traditionally just sold a product in a variety of industries. Defense, consumer goods, financial services, healthcare, industrials – each industry has worked through the pain of moving from a "free" service to a paid service.

Too technical? Okay. How about the concept of a wedding planner? Or a personal shopper? Or an Uber driver? When I was growing up, these jobs didn't really exist. If you rented the wedding hall, someone would help you plan it as a part of the cost of the rental. The idea of having someone shop for you simply wasn't even considered in the 1970s as I was growing up. And if you needed to share a ride, it was either a friend or a thumb in the early 1980s. Being paid to give someone a lift only happened in a taxi.

The coolest part about the service economy is its cadence and opportunity. What you sell as a service is limited only by your ability to think and act. Unlike a new computer from a manufacturer that requires years to design and produce, service innovation happens at the speed of thought and is an incredibly exciting and dynamic product development world to compete in.

But with great freedom and innovation comes great responsibility.

***

It's not every day you get to work with a self-proclaimed Jedi of Privacy, but I have had that honor! Michelle Dennedy is a pioneer in the field of privacy, having served as Chief Privacy Officer for Cisco, Chief Privacy Officer at McAfee/Intel, VP for Security and Privacy Solutions at

Oracle, Chief Data Governance Officer within Cloud Computing, and Chief Privacy Officer at Sun Microsystems. She's also a lawyer and the coauthor of two books, *The Privacy Engineer's Manifesto* and *The Privacy Engineer's Companion.*

As you consider providing services in the market, in the current world of "data monetization," you have to consider privacy and its implications for your company. As an example, Michelle and I talked a bit about healthcare in a post-COVID world:

> Going forward we're going to start seeing what is appropriate for medicine that's done remotely. I think we're going to see a huge spike in new services that can be economically delivered for things like mental healthcare, eldercare, things where it's really difficult, expensive, and logistically hard to get people to these doctors' offices without harming them or exposing them to a greater risk of infections. Or even them infecting other people, causing a whole different economic problem.

She's right. The services you will see offered in response to the emerging COVID crisis will create a new standard of care, and many companies are racing to serve that segment.

Oliver Richards, our Chief Growth Officer and SVP for Healthcare and Life Sciences practice, talked about the future offerings that will collide physical product, software, and data in the very near term:

> It starts with better, longer-term patient management and more personalized medicine, where you combine data streams. I mean chronic care management is a huge issue right now, trying to track a patient over years and decades and preventing disease progression and identifying risks as things progress. I think there's a ton of value in telehealth solutions assisting in that process. Longer term, I'm excited when I think about the next-gen sequencing [NGS] and how cheap that's gotten over the last decade or so. I joked a decade ago that it's kind of like Moore's Law now applied to NGS. I think you're getting to the point where you can do whole genome sequencing or targeted sequencing really cheaply. And then once you start combining genetics plus monitoring plus other factors, what you can actually do gets pretty cool.

Michelle and Oliver are talking about next-level offerings, and they illustrate that when you consider what you will offer to the market, you have to do it through both a goods and services focal plane.

There is a truth, though. In both manufacturing and services, there are generally incentives to leverage existing offerings as long as possible. Economies of scale come as you grow the business in manufacturing, and the experience curve comes into play for service offerings. They both basically argue the same thing – that the more you do something, the cheaper it is to do. If that's true, revisiting our profit equation from the Introduction (Profit = Revenue – Cost), then if I decrease cost, I increase profit.

The corollary truth of the market is that over time, almost all goods and services become stale, so their price drops. If the price drops faster than the cost drops, then the margin drops. Not good.

Bill Gates said it best. *"In three years, every product my company makes will be obsolete. The only question is whether we will make them obsolete or somebody else will."*[1]

There is always a tension between selling as much as possible of what you currently make in the market and selling something new. As a rule, there is generally more profit in selling more of the same if you can maintain your price point. But commoditization over time as new entrants start to play erodes price and margin, so that leads to the rollout of new goods and services. You hear quite a bit about market disruption and innovation. Intuitively that leads to the notion of new products and services entering an existing and established market. Sometimes that disruption comes from new market entrants, sometimes by existing competitors. Number two wants to be number one, so they change what they are selling. Of course, the money to develop the NEW disrupting good or service comes from the sale of EXISTING products and services for this competitor, so the management of a portfolio of offerings is the typical need for each business. This is classically done as part of product lifecycle management.

Selling existing products/services is generally a more profitable, lower risk exercise. Existing products have already gone through design, engineering, packaging, marketing, and production. There is no development timeline to worry about. There is no new training for your sales team. There is less risk that the market won't exist.

But prices erode over time, so new products are needed. New products are very risky. Depending on the type of product or service, there can be significant investment of time, materials, and capital in both production and market creation.

Note

1. QuoteFancy.com, https://quotefancy.com/quote/775634/Bill-Gates-In-three-years-every-product-my-company-makes-will-be-obsolete-The-only.

5

What BUSINESS MODEL Will I Use?

About a decade ago, there was a fundamental shift in the physics of competition among publicly traded corporations. They began to allow changes in their traditional business models.

The first time I really dug into this was helping a client study the emerging market for energy services. Companies were being merged to create super-ESCOs, or energy services companies. These were large companies that combined excellence in the provision and management of massive HVAC infrastructure with financial risk management. Let me say this more clearly.

Imagine you run the infrastructure for a skyscraper in Manhattan: 50 stories, 200 units, 200 tenants. Manhattan is in the northeastern US and experiences every climate imaginable. So it's critical that as a top-notch landlord, you have to keep tenants at a constant 71 degrees, winter, spring, summer, or fall. There was really only one way to do that before the late 1990s. You bought and maintained a massive heating, ventilation, and cooling (HVAC) system.

What you learn from studying landlords in Manhattan who own skyscrapers is that they are fairly sophisticated financially, and they know exactly what they spend to finance that equipment on a monthly basis and the amount of electricity and maintenance cost that they spend to provide that service to their tenants.

For the sake of illustration, let's say that the AC units cost $750,000 to buy, $250,000 to install, and $40,000 a month to run. So a cool $1 million to buy and half a million per year to operate. Those are real dollars that get even more real as the product reaches a point called "end of life." That's when the equipment fails and needs to be replaced.

In the 1990s, at end of life it was a very, very painful decision to spend to replace the equipment, only to find that costs went up, and the cost to make it integrate/retrofit with the old system made it even more expensive than the original install!

Then came the ESCOs. The ESCO salesperson would sit with you, go over the CapEx and OpEx (capital expenditure – the cost of buying the equipment; operating expenditure – the cost of implementing and operating the equipment) and convert that into a standard monthly payment. But it wasn't just financing your cost. Let's say that when you average the cost of your purchase and operations over a 10-year time frame it's $80,000 a month. The ESCO would guarantee you that your property would maintain at between say 68 and 72 degrees 98% of the time for $70,000 a month.

That's a $10k/month savings for your building. Would you go for it?

What the ESCO didn't share is that they ran their own numbers, and with their level of expertise and by using the most efficient technology, they could provide that "service level" for $60,000 a month. So, they would make $120,000 a year on your contract. Over a 10-year time frame that's $1.2 million – that's a good business.

The other hidden gem in this example is that they are still acquiring the system from their vendor of choice, which drove potential market share gains for partners as well.

Our analysis of this market led to a major acquisition by our client.

This was the first real change in the business model of a traditional business that I encountered. I was intrigued, and I kept a sharp eye out for other change that was occurring.

Tom Klenke has the dubious honor of being my roommate at Darden. He is a fellow sailor, pilot, and outdoorsman who is also a successful serial entrepreneur. He still owes me for introducing him to his amazing wife, Naomi, a fellow Darden grad who has been at his side and a true partner throughout his journey. Tom was at the forefront of the "as a service" business-model disruption, and I got him to talk about it. The story goes that a few years after business school, after successful stints at both Symantec and Intuit, Tom and his partner Mark Pizzolato created what would become one of the top three companies providing mass emailing services to his clients in the late 1990s. In fact, Tom and Mark are arguably the inventors of that most useful part of every digital campaign: the unsubscribe button! During our interview, we talked about how he was able to use a service-based offering to create scale in his market.

> Starting an internet-based service business was clear to me because of what I was doing at Intuit. One of my jobs was helping to be the voice of Intuit North for building its big data warehouse, which was this very expensive, strategic project Intuit embarked on. But that was a small part of my job and the rest of my job was helping the Intuit North folks get their direct mail pieces out. In order to do that at the time you used to have to pull the data out of order processing mainframes on tapes, literally tapes like "Space 1999," and ship them to the data processing houses in Chicago. I was the interface to working among my internal customers, the product marketers, and these external service bureaus that would take all the data and slice it and dice it and get it ready to mail. When the email thing came up, I thought of it like a service bureau, but for email. I had many connections with other high-tech direct marketers because we had worked together in the world's most highly educated migrant workforce that is Silicon Valley. When we got eClass up and running it was an easy sale to the direct marketers saying, "It's just mail, but it's electronic." Since I was talking to other direct marketers, they were used to working with service bureaus so it was easy for them.

This wasn't just a new offering. Tom used familiarity with service bureau billing and technology evolution to drive scale in his market, and he emerged as a leading early player in the "as a service" domain. No surprise, others were watching this variable of business model become more and more important. Don Scales talked about his experience:

> Everything's changed. When I first started working, there was no such thing as recurring revenue . . . but then software got big and then recurring started coming in. And now in this business, that's what they value. The markets want to value predictable revenue streams and so **now** the focus is on how much of your revenue is recurring. Clearly if you can get into a company that has a high degree of recurring revenue, life's a lot easier.

Traditional business models have been under attack over the past decade. No longer is the notion of a sale simple. We have aaS or "as a service" offerings of all shapes and sizes. Pay for performance, fee for service, consumption-based models abound, and they are limited only by the ability and willingness of a company to absorb financial risk.

I was a budding growth strategist during the introduction of smartphones. I was lucky enough to be involved in studying the commercialization opportunities for WAP (wireless access protocol), which was the foundation for phones to surf the web. Literally we helped define what the ability to connect to the internet was worth on your phone. At the time, phone displays were nothing like today, and we had to come up with a way to value the offering. We succeeded in helping our client bring this to market, and when that happened, an entirely new market segment was created. Starting in 2000, thanks to WAP, Motorola, Samsung, Nokia all competed through wireless carriers to offer their own version of the smartphone. It was a cutthroat model, where companies hired software designers to create killer apps through the software capability of their phone. *Killer app* is a term to describe applications that drive mass adoption. Back then, the notion of a calendar function or GPS navigation on a phone simply didn't exist, and companies were working hard to create their own unique offerings.

This was the key differentiator in the war among carriers to attract customers and to minimize churn in their base. Billions were spent trying to figure out the best applications to drive differentiation and ideally a higher rate of customer loyalty and spend. This trench warfare continued until Steve Jobs entered the market in 2007 with the iPhone.

Obviously, the phone itself was a new product, with more memory, screen, battery life, and user interface. But it didn't stop there – a year after the phone was introduced, Apple disrupted the market's closed business model, democratizing the production of applications. This created an entirely new revenue stream for the company – the App store.

Fundamentally, Jobs offered an alternative to closed, unique apps on carrier's cell phone by creating a marketplace for independent developers to write applications. No one at that point monetized the software capabilities of the phone – it was a giveaway included in the cost of service.

Apple not only differentiated the iPhone through the breadth of applications that could be accessed but also they created an entirely new revenue source. They built the ecosystem, gave away the development tools, administered the marketing and sale of apps, taking a fee of 30% of sales. It was simple, disruptive, and sustainable. In short, it stood the market on its ear overnight and had a material impact on the return of Apple to mainstream growth.

I recently was talking to a senior executive at Microsoft during a touch-base call. He suggested that due to some careful fiscal management by the current CFO, they were in great shape to make some inorganic acquisitions. I offered the opinion that while that was true, really, they were in good shape because in 2010 Microsoft was forced to answer the 2006 game-changing launch of Google Gmail and their subsequent suite of Google apps. Office 365 was a fundamental, existential bet the company made, with a subscription-based offering that shifted the revenue model from the traditional software sale (~$800 for MS Office shrink-wrapped) to a ~$39.95 recurring monthly payment. A move from CapEx to OpEx. If not for this change, I believe that today Microsoft would be in a world of hurt. Most aaS offerings represent a disruption to market incumbents, and are currently being universally considered across markets and offerings.

Athena Murphy is the VP of Transformation and Chief of Staff to the CEO of Juniper Networks. A graduate of UC Berkeley, and a former senior product manager and corporate strategy practitioner at Intel, Athena is a student of evolution and recognizes the challenges of business model disruption to mature, established competitors.

It's an uphill battle to get your customer to all of a sudden pay a different way. You need to make the shift to either a new customer base or a new geography. You need to figure out where you can conceptually start from scratch instead of trying to disrupt someone who's been getting something for free for a long time. Just because you decided to shift to revenue services model doesn't mean your customers are going to agree. "By the way, now I'm going to charge you for that service" – that doesn't go over well.

There are all kinds of new models that have been considered over time – joint venture, fee for service, time and materials, performance-based, risk-sharing, aaS, profit sharing . . . the list is a pretty long and inventive one. Business model innovation is one area where smaller companies and their more flexible mindset seem to shine, although there are models that are best served by companies of scale.

In this world, you run across people who are what you wish you could be. People who you realize, down to their marrow, have a strong value system, work ethic, an appreciation of their strengths and weaknesses, and can bring others along with them. I first met John Seebeck in 1992. A few weeks ago I spent some time on the phone with his son Lyle, brainstorming about some areas he wants to pursue as an entrepreneur . . . Lyle was but a bump in his mother Elizabeth's belly when John and I graduated from Darden in 1994. I think it's safe to say he's a chip off the old block.

In his current role, John leads the e-commerce business for CDW, an $18 billion global leader that sells all things tech through an e-commerce channel, from computers to SaaS, to just about anyone you can think of, from people to businesses to government. Prior to working at CDW, John led a revolution in the business of one of my favorite stores, Crate & Barrel:

> I joined Crate & Barrel in the early part of 2001. My title was Senior Internet Manager. The company had about 2% of sales being run through their website. [The] company had launched a website in April of '99. The CEO, under duress from his son, allowed the launch of a website and everybody at Crate & Barrel hated the idea . . . they saw the company as high touch. Customer service oriented. Get people into the stores, get people immersed in the beauty of the stores and why

the hell would someone buy a piece of furniture online, right? So my job there was really kind of convincing people that this was a good idea, and porting over the entire business to online. When I got there it was at 1 to 2% [of sales]. And when I left it was about 45% of total [sales].

Reread that. We all take e-commerce for granted. A standard part of our life. Reality is, it is a relatively new disruption of the business model in retail. John transformed Crate & Barrel by changing its business model. From 2% to 45% of sales. He started as a forced hire, with a manager title, and ended up the direct report of the CEO with a title of Vice President e-Commerce. I'm not sure what percentage of sales they have today, but John led in their continued dominance of a really tough market. What was really interesting about this example was why Crate & Barrel hired John in the first place. They were having their own business disrupted by competitors!

Well . . . our customers were shopping elsewhere because we didn't have the ability to serve them online. Our customers were demanding it. Some were very loyal and will just keep shopping with you. But some were going to go to Williams Sonoma and their group of companies.

Another one of my favorite people is Sheri Dodd. I've known and worked with Sheri for over a decade, and she's the kind of professional you hope you can be. Thoughtful, honest, smart, experienced, decisive, kind, funny. The list could go on, but I think you get the drift. Did I say accomplished? Sheri is the VP and GM of Medtronic's Care Management Services Division, which is on the front line of the company's remote care initiative. We first met and worked together when Sheri was the VP for Worldwide Health Economics and Reimbursement for Ethicon at Johnson & Johnson. She's also a veteran of the World Health Organization where she supported their Eastern Mediterranean office. Sheri is also a graduate of the London School of Economics with a Master's of Science in Health Economics and a Master's of Science in Epidemiology from the London School of Hygiene and Tropical Medicine. A native of Montana, Sheri is a great blend of frontier strength and ingenuity mixed with the formal education and sophistication that only British higher education can provide. Sheri was nice enough to take the time to participate in this book, and she shared some advanced insight on outcome risk–based business models. Note – an outcome risk–based business model is one where you only get paid if you perform to a level you negotiate initially. It's pretty daunting unless you know you can really back up your claim, which Sheri usually does:

> We've got some really bold ROI programs in our remote patient monitoring business where we essentially went to commercial payers and said if you allow us to select and risk stratify the patients and you allow our nurses to do the initial triage of the patient symptom and vital signs data that's transmitted through our home-based remote monitoring program, we will guarantee a certain ROI at the end of one year in terms of reduction in claims costs . . . What we found through this is sometimes you're ahead of your customer.
> Anytime you enter a new business model you're not an expert at it either, so you have got a lot of learnings and I think part of the beauty of that is if you are experimenting, you are naturally going to be ahead of your competitors if they're not experimenting . . . that if you're learning, you already are generating value that is not easily quantified from an immediate financial standpoint but it's critical for growth.
> In operationalizing this new model we were wildly successful in some areas and had gaps in other areas. We know more about our targeted patient population than ever and we got paid along the way. We didn't have to buy deidentified claims data and model potential benefit, we didn't have to wonder about stratification methods. We are in a learning lab right now and we see the talent development happening with our own teams . . . We have more customer and product performance insights than we've ever had and insights that we are using to improve our program. The hardest part is getting enough runway to prove success or failure and to quantify how learnings brought value and saved the company time and money.

Sheri does a great job illustrating why "What business model will I use?" is one of our four key questions. There are so many implicit and explicit challenges of a new business model, not the least of which is that it's new! You are learning with your client what works and what doesn't.

I'll give you a final example. At Beacon, I believe we are the world's leading thinkers on growth strategy, and we are constantly being asked by our clients to consider models of recurring revenue for our firm. We currently sell almost entirely fixed-fee projects and offer a guarantee on our work. That guarantee model has been disruptive in our industry for the two decades we have been in business, and it is based on best practices I was able to distill from my years in the industry. We are able to do in 6 to 10 weeks what other firms want 9 months to do. Our advice is better because we are growth specialists, we have the best data, our counsel is pragmatic, offered in a timely fashion, and the results are more successful. Our model, and its results, have driven our performance of 80% to 90% recurring revenue from existing clients against industry juggernauts like McKinsey, BCG, and Bain. However, we are constantly asked by clients to provide retainers, risk sharing, even multiyear contracts. Today, we are being asked to move into an adjacency that will have us compete with titans in the industry who are purely focused on market sizing and wield incredible influence in the investor community. To support this, we will have to engage in a new business model – annual support, multiyear staffing, recurring revenue stream. Sounds great, but when I started Beacon, I saw the bloat that those dynamics bring to services organizations. When you know you have revenue coming in, you don't work as hard to earn it. I deliberately structured our approach to prevent this. We have a Special Forces mindset. Immerse, go deep, be focused and fast, solve, and move on. As we go forward with this client, because of their strategic value, I'm working to embrace this new opportunity. However, I'm going to make sure that we engineer risks of complacency out of our model. It will be a learning experience, and like Sheri, I'll value the process.

This is a very important lesson as you think about the *why* behind changes companies make. Sometimes they are offensive, sometimes they are defensive, sometimes they are opportunistic. At all times, they are seeking to provide competitive advantage, and there is nothing more powerful in your strategy toolkit right now than your ability to change your business model.

CHAPTER

6

The Growth Framework: The 16 Ways a Company Can Grow

In this chapter, we expand the Four Key Questions into the 16 Growth Pathways. A critical part of our process, this powerful instrument helps you frame the growth challenge in a clean, repeatable, logical way. Having a tool to exhaustively consider how you could grow in a simple, direct way is critical to success.

When you consider the Four Key Questions as a series of choices, and limit the possible outcomes to new or existing, you get a powerful model: the Growth Framework

Before digging into the framework, it can help to answer the Four Key Questions, which largely determine planning success and failure. Practically, the way that they are best used is to consider them conversationally:

1. What % of planned revenues will come from existing clients?

2. What % of planned revenues will come from existing geographies/locations?

3. What % of planned revenues will come from existing goods and services?

4. What % of planned revenues will come from existing business models?

These are very simple questions for the team to wrap their heads around. Simple is powerful, and by answering these questions you can evaluate the best ways to achieve your objective. Because these present more questions than can be considered in the typical 2×2 format, we need a new framework to help us plan for success and help us talk about what happens when the four questions collide.

I spent time thinking through both my project and personal experience, reviewing success and failure, cost and reward, natural and disruptive growth. It became clear that the four key questions were the most important areas a growth strategist had to get right.

So, a drill. Don't overthink it. Simply answer the following questions:

What % of revenue will come from existing customers?   _____%
What % of revenue will come from existing geographies/locations? _____%
What % of revenues will come from existing goods and services?   _____%
What % of revenues will come from existing business models?   _____%

Got that? I refer to that as a Top-Down Drill, one of two ways we will work through planning.

Now, put your answers to the side (we will come back to them in subsequent chapters). For now, let's look at how the Four Key Questions turn into our Growth Framework.

When you build a framework to evaluate a problem, whether it's which house to buy or which school to attend, you have to start with the end in mind. What are the design rules that you are building into the tool you want to create? In my case, it took quite a bit of thought to develop: hours drawing and erasing different potential formats over the period of a few weeks in between project work. Self-critique, trial and error . . . but it was really fun to see it come together.

I had a few design rules in mind:

- It had to be helpful.
- It had to be simple and easy to use.
- It had to be logical.
- It had to be based on learnings from both success and failure in markets.
- It had to be exhaustive – to consider all potential ways a company could grow.
- It had to be intuitive to a user once explained.
- It had to be financial, with ROI chops.
- It had to quickly show traps/red herrings.
- It had to leave room for change.
- It had to be time bounded.
- It had to be practical.

When you order the Four Key Questions in order of risk/reward, they create a decision tree framework that both makes sense and is a useful way to simply think through the challenges of developing your growth strategy (see Figure 6.1).

Take your time and look at this framework. It is in the format of a decision tree. It presents 16 mutually exclusive and collectively exhaustive pathways to consider every potential source of growth for any business in existence.

Growth Framework

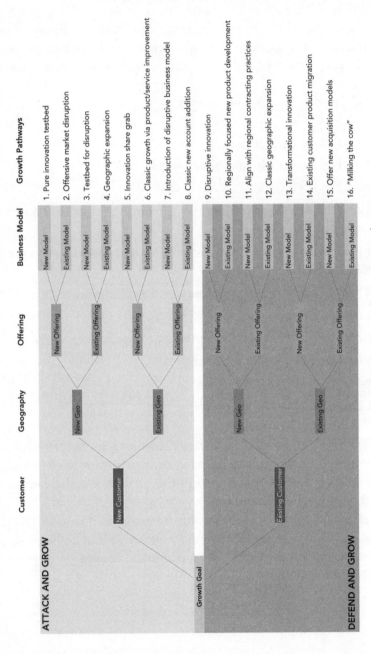

FIGURE 6.1   Growth Framework

Growth Pathways Defined

Let's go through the 16 Growth Pathways in more detail. We will start with the broad Defend and Grow group of 8, focusing on existing customers.

Defend and Grow Pathways

Companies of scale don't have the luxury of unfettered behavior when growing their business. Growth usually must not be at the cost of existing relationships. Current clients have to be protected and also serve as the primary source of growth for most businesses. It's a paradox. Existing clients limit what you can do, but they also generally allow you to grow faster than someone trying to attract new customers. The first half of our pathways acknowledge this reality under the header of Defend and Grow.

Pathway 16: Milking the Cow

This is the baseline condition for most companies. Classically understood, this is simply companies doing what they do well with customers they know, in current locations with a typical contracting approach. This is also typically where significant operating profit comes from and requires little investment to support.

Examples:

- *P&G selling original Crest toothpaste*
- *Shell selling petrol*
- *Starbucks selling a cup of coffee*
- *Apple selling last year's iPhone*
- *Basically any company doing what they did last year*

Pathway 15: Offer New Acquisition Models

Typically a response to competitive pressure. This pathway is usually forced on a company in response to a disruptive acquisition offering by competitors. I say typically because it's very difficult to change business models that are working well for a company. Now, there are companies who reinvent themselves, but for the most part, this will be a reactive move.

Examples:

- Michael Dell's early 2020 announcement "All offerings As-a-service"
- 2019 Nike announcement of the Nike Adventure Club, provides kids 2–10 a subscription service for new shoes
- 2019 Ikea rollout of furniture leasing
- 1962 Rolls Royce "power by the hour" business model, charging airlines for engines by their hours used instead of outright sale

Pathway 14: Existing Customer Product Migration

This happens at the core of most companies as a normal course of business. You develop a new product or service and offer it to your existing customers. Whether a new dish on your menu if you are a restaurateur, or a new function in your software update, giving your customers something new is at the core of longevity for businesses since the beginning of commerce.

Examples:

- *Uber Eats being offered to existing Uber customers 5 years after its inaugural ride*
- *Every new smartphone you've ever bought through your existing carrier*
- *A new pair of sunglasses from your favorite brand*
- *That new Caramel Brule Latte that Starbucks is offering this holiday season*

There is an endless list of examples that we've all experienced.

Pathway 13: Transformational Innovation

Literally, this pathway will transform how you engage with your customers. You will offer them *new products* that they can *acquire in new ways*. Microsoft 365 or HPE's Greenlake is a great example of this. New products are being provided to customers through an aaS or consumption-based model. They are transforming how they engage with clients.

Example: Rami Rahim, CEO of Juniper Networks, offered the following story:

> *In an industry that's continuing to change and evolve – where your customers have big ambitions and you're developing innovative products that differ from the old way of doing things – it becomes more important than ever to think about and plan for the future. Juniper has developed enhanced services capabilities. We are no longer just shipping value in the form of a box that sits on a crate that's delivered to a customer. We are now shipping value in the form of hardware and software separately and increasing through SaaS (software as a service) and it all has to work together – and our customer skills and capabilities are not necessarily as big as what their ambitions are, right? So in order to help them with that, we've had to think about offering services and solutions – and that has worked very well for us.*

Rahim is steering Juniper to offer a new set of capabilities that have driven transformational innovation in the markets he has traditionally served. Instead of offering just hardware, Juniper offers new kinds of hardware, software, and services to his customers using new business models that embrace the consumption economy. This is powerful stuff and exactly what his company needs to grow in a tough market. I can't wait to see his progress in markets served as he executes this strategy.

Pathway 12: Classic Geographic Expansion

This pathway is accessed when a company expands its footprint. There are a number of ways this happens, depending on your business structure, but in this pathway we consider the actual expansion of physical infrastructure. So opening a new storefront, or a regional office, or entering an entirely new country is what we are talking about in Pathway 12. The risks are many – financial, legal, regulatory, economic, HR. This pathway is most often triggered when a company feels limited on either clients or recruiting. This is when you believe you need a physical presence to access to a new pool of either customers or employees. This is often accomplished through acquisition.

Examples:

- McDonalds has used geographic expansion to scale to over 31,000 worldwide locations.
- Amazon Web Services has expanded to provide global coverage of its AWS offerings, most recently at time of printing announcing expansion of footprint in India to support growth.

Pathway 11: Align with Regional Contracting Practices

This is generally a business-to-business (B2B) play with very specific requirements. An example is a component supplier to a multinational corporation. In selling within a new region to the same customer, the government may require different behaviors on business structure/ownership, currency used, repatriation of profit to HQ company . . . there are a number of things that can drive this. Making sure you understand the risk/reward benefit of this approach is critical.

Example:

In 2010, Sikorsky Aircraft entered into a JV with Tata Advanced Systems to manufacture and assemble cabins for the S-92 helicopter at their new manufacturing plant in India. The move was not to lower manufacturing costs, but to help encourage local sales while supporting their existing production goals. Though it preceded the "Make in India" rules established in 2014, the JV helped fulfill the Indian government's requirement for large government purchases to undergo a portion of domestic manufacturing.[1]

Pathway 10: Regionally Focused New Product Development

This pathway acknowledges the diversity of culture, preference, physiology, and competitive landscape in different geographies. Simple examples can be found in things like the power supply infrastructure in different countries – 110V versus 220V. Again, since this pathway deals with existing customers, in the B2B world, this would involve supplier or partner relationships with multinational corporations. In communications, insurance, and banking, you also see examples where consumers travel around the world, and they expect their services to follow them, requiring new relationships with partner providers internationally.

Example:

In 2019 DB Schenker won a GHS (Global Heavyweight Service) award to serve the DoD. In order to support this mission they built a new classified warehouse in Virginia. This was an existing customer for DB Schenker, though a new geography, as they had to expand their physical infrastructure. This is also a new offering for DB as the GHS award allows them to transport more products and more fully service the DoD, and these services are sold via a traditional model.

Pathway 9: Disruptive Innovation

The tricky part of this one is that you are pursuing an existing customer, in a new geography, with a new offering and a new model. New offering/new model pathways are always disruptive by definition, but when you add in the geographic risk of execution and the risk of damaging or changing customer relationships it becomes more difficult. Examples in the services world abound. A classic management consulting firm offers new technical services on a performance contracting basis in a new geography to support a client's international growth. It's only one swim lane over from the core offerings of the company, but it still has the potential to change the perception of the brand, what it does, and how it's acquired within the larger client. This is a glass half empty/half full question – it's neither good nor bad depending on your goals, but it is very, very tricky to execute well and a high-risk approach.

Example:

In 1983 Sam Walton opened the first Sam's Club. Walmart had already been around for almost 20 years, so this served existing customers, but through a limited expansion of physical infrastructure. This was a new offering. The store sold bulk goods, often still packaged on crates/ shipping pallets, and was a new model, as shoppers had to be members and pay membership subscription fees.

Attack and Grow

At this point, we shift gears and focus on the eight Attack and Grow pathways. These are focused on pure new growth initiatives that are coming from new clients. The eight Defend and Grow pathways we just discussed rely on existing customers for growth. The Attack and

Grow pathways are focused on new customer acquisition. Unless you are creating an entirely new market (rare), you will be taking a customer from someone else.

The Attack and Grow pathways are a heavier lift and potentially longer timeline. This is clear as you consider the traditional marketing and sales challenges associated with new customer acquisition: making new customers aware of your existence and capability, creating interest in learning about what you do, developing trust in your capability to serve, generating desire to acquire your goods/services, and, finally, closing the deal.

Pathway 8: Classic New Account Addition

Every business uses this pathway as either its first or second priority as it works to grow. Start-ups focus solely on this initially, younger companies put significant focus on it, older companies look for 10% to 20% of revenues to come from this. This is the grind of acquiring a new customer. Creating awareness, desire, demand, and all the other parts of new customer acquisition are focused on this activity. Depending on market maturity, acquiring a new customer can be easy or hard. For mature markets, you are "taking away" customers from someone else, while in young markets you are "creating customers." Expect this to be a part of every growth strategy you develop. The other thing to consider is that sometimes this demand is due to factors outside your control. Regulatory change, competitor divestiture, or shutdown – the behaviors of public figures and the new definition of cool in the social media realm can make your existing products suddenly in demand by new customers. Think 3M for masks in the COVID crisis once the current administration approved N95 masks for use as PPE (personal protective equipment) by clinicians. Kevin Watters talked about acquiring new customers in the banking industry:

Kevin: We always thought about when kids were eligible. Ideally, you want someone's first checking account to be with you, because chances are if your parents banked with Chase they got you a Chase account, right? Authorized user on their credit card.

Cliff: I still remember, it was a big deal, going down to the bank and getting your own checking account.

Kevin: Chances are if we get you like that we will have you the rest of your life. If you move to a city and there's a Chase there, we've got you. You're not going anywhere.

Kevin's quote shows why companies value the addition of a new customer so much. If you do it right, there isn't just a transactional value, there is a lifetime value.

Pathway 7: Introduction of Disruptive Business Model

This is typically a reactive pathway, driven by changes in the larger competitive landscape or a more creative, short-term "try something new" attempt to secure new customers. "Get three months free if you buy now" is a short-term change from the norm (which is a monthly charge) that you would see used under this pathway. This is something unusual/new for your business that gains new revenues from new clients. There's typically an *"offer only valid for new customers"* tag line associated with promotions like this. Longer-term change would be caused if you were facing new competition that was altering the standard practice in the market. Note that you have to look at the model through your own corporate lens, not what would be generally deemed as disruptive in other industries.

Examples:

- *TD Bank "Beyond Checking" $300 cash bonus for new customers*
- *AT&T $300 Visa reward for new customers with AT&T TV and internet*
- *First-time home-buyer programs offered by a state*

Pathway 6: Classic Growth via Product/Service Improvement

I could have called this pathway "build a better mousetrap," because that is essentially what you do to drive growth here. You attract new clients because you have a product that they really want. By making things better, faster, cheaper (or any one of a number of other design parameters) you win business. Think about the smartphone you own.

Examples:

If you are a loyal iPhone or Android user who has switched from one to the other at least once in your life, then you've followed this pathway. What about the move a consumer makes from a Ford to a Chevy or from Delta to American. Transactionally, every time you've gone to a new brand or product, you've demonstrated the power of this pathway. That's why companies spend billions on new product development. Literally, billions – each year! Any one of the leaders interviewed in this book has a personal war chest of successful revenue generation from this pathway.

Pathway 5: Innovation Share Grab

This pathway is incredibly disruptive in an existing market. Innovation Share Grab is when you acquire a new customer through a new product and new business model.

Example:

So many great examples of this, but one that many can relate to is Google Mail and Google Apps taking share from Microsoft. You have to remember that Google was a search engine that suddenly had an offering for Mail that challenged Microsoft Outlook. As Google added applications including word processing to their offering, Microsoft had to take notice as they began to take away accounts from their core customers. People would use Microsoft at work but Google for personal communications and documents. Google was brilliant in their rollout of Gmail, where they limited the number of free accounts offered, and for a while a Gmail account was a status symbol among tech-savvy consumers. The double whammy of a new product and a "free" offering took a major chunk out of Microsoft and drove the creation of Office 365, resulting in eventual long-term success for Microsoft. As you consider growth, you have to think about the power this pathway has for you to enter mature existing markets. This is a nuclear weapon in your arsenal and one that always has to be considered. The most evolved thinking will be to obsolete yourself . . . but that is so counterintuitive – why would you do that? Survival is one reason.

Pathway 4: Geographic Expansion

This is the first of the four pathways that include a consideration of entry to new geographies. It's incredibly difficult to enter a new location, and you have to be sure that you model out your assumptions of return as you consider it. Is the market big enough? Do I understand the requirements for market entry? Is my brand recognized within this geography?

Example:

I did a project for credit while I was in B-School at Darden. It was a life experience that I remember well to this day. The year was 1993, and communism had come to an end in Eastern Europe. It was a tumultuous time there, as commercial, government, and black market entities interacted in the development of each country's economy. Jack Daniels had been getting into the Eastern European market through black market channels, and we were asked to assess whether or not Brown Foreman (the parent company of Jack Daniels) should establish a more formal channel to the market. After crawling across Poland, through an incredible number of both normal bars and venues that would have been at home in Manhattan, my teammates and I decided that the answer was no. The brand was protected at a premium price, the economies hadn't yet developed enough to sustain general consumption, and Brown Foreman's money was better spent developing brands somewhere else. Understand this – there is GREAT value in avoiding a bad investment, and in this case I think we gave good advice. That said, this pathway is a classic model for growth and one that should be considered.

Pathway 3: Test Bed for Disruption

This is one of my favorite if most misunderstood and underappreciated pathways. When you enter a new geography, you are by definition "physically" away from the core business. This environment is amazingly important for growth. It's like the difference in personal growth that can be found in going away to school versus living at home while you attend college. Moving out is freeing! It allows you to test and try new things with the safety net of home if you need it. For business, it's the same thing – when you are in a new geography, assuming you serve a different customer community, you can really try new and disruptive things. You can learn a new way of conducting business that can then be brought back into the core of your business. View geographic expansion as the opportunity to learn about disruption WITHOUT disrupting your fundamental business.

Examples:

- *In 2018, Dunkin Donuts began to roll out a series of new locations with new, modernized services and offerings. Among these are cold beverages on tap, Dunkin on Demand digital kiosks to handle customer orders independently of staff, and dedicated mobile pickup and drive-through lanes. These new locations are targeted at new customers, in new geographies, is an existing offering from Dunkin Donuts, but sold via the On Demand Kiosks, which is a new model.[2]*
- *In the late 1990s and early 2000s Kodak Co. was transitioning its focus to the Chinese market. Part of its strategy was gifting over 5,000 traditional cameras to poor and rural regions of the country where very few households owned one, in hopes that increasing familiarity and awareness of the device would drive consumption. These were new customers in a new geography, was an existing offering from Kodak, but was offered via a new model.[3]*

Pathway 2: Offensive Market Disruption

This is an attack pathway to take share from incumbents in a new geographic market with a new and desired product or service. This pathway is a predatory play, especially for late entrants to a market. Using a new offering to take share in an entirely new geography is a classic move from growing companies.

Examples:

- *A great example is the entry of Starbucks into the China market. In 1999 they built their first store in the largely tea-drinking market, and over 13 years they opened over 550 stores in 48 cities. This was an immense success that allowed them to take share in a developed country.*
- *Another great example is Red Bull in the US. Red Bull, counter to much popular belief, is not a US company. They are an Austrian company! The US was an offensive market disruption and significant growth opportunity for them, which has obviously worked out: Red Bull is one of the most recognized drink brands in the market.*

Pathway 1: Pure Innovation Test Bed

This is the final pathway in the framework, and one that has many values and many risks. Let's start with the risks – this is THE riskiest Growth Pathway. New customers who don't know you. New geographies with all of the inherent challenge of operation. A new offering that may or may not be attractive in the market. Finally, the challenge of a new business model, its implementation, and support. Because this is so risky and so carefully pursued, we deem it a test bed activity. You'd never look to see a significant amount of revenue from this pathway in the first year, and by the time years 3 to 5 roll around these revenues are part of your existing models, existing geos, existing products. The value in this approach is to discretely try new things that could evolve your core business with customers that really impact nothing if it doesn't work out. This is the ultimate test bed/lab environment.

Example:

In 2014, Evernote launched a localized version of its app in China. As part of the product's strategy, Evernote localized the content, including integration, into the popular Chinese platforms WeChat and Weibo. They also adapted the prices and services offered and began accepting Alipay mobile payments. Finally, to help mitigate lag and slow speeds, Evernote built local servers in China. With this strategy, Evernote was targeting new customers in a new geography, which included the expansion of physical infrastructure, with a new offering, and a new mobile payment model.[4]

Some Examples to Consider

Okay I know that was a pretty detailed walkthrough. Let's keep that page bookmarked for reference but move into examples that consider the two guardrails of business: large enterprise and small business.

Let's start with a run through a typical company in the Fortune 500. If you consider the company at an aggregate level, the following is likely true:

Growth Framework Output

Property of Cliff Farrah/The Beacon Group – not for distribution

Created for *Fortune 200 Company X*

Color coding represents relative attractiveness of each pathway.

The darker the revenue percentage and target revenues are, the better it is for you. Medium gray pathways require discussion. Optimal pathways are bolded.

Customer	Geography	Offering	Business Model	Percentage of Revenues from each Pathway	Target Revenues for each Pathway	Growth Pathways
NEW GROWTH						
		20% New Offering	0% New Model	0%	$ —	1. Pure innovation testbed
	0% New Geo		100% Existing Model	0%	$ —	2. Offensive market disruption
		80% Existing Offering	0% New Model	0%	$ —	3. Testbed for disruption
20% New Customer			100% Existing Model	0%	$ —	4. Geographic expansion
		20% New Offering	0% New Model	0%	$ —	5. Innovation share grab
	100% Existing Geo		100% Existing Model	4.00%	$ 40,000	6. Classic growth via product/service improvement
		80% Existing Offering	0% New Model	0%	$ —	7. Introduction of disruptive business model
			100% Existing Model	16.00%	$ 160,000	8. Classic new account addition
DEFEND AND GROW						
		20% New Offering	0% New Model	0%	$ —	9. Disruptive innovation
	0% New Geo		100% Existing Model	0%	$ —	10. Regionally focused new product development
		80% Existing Offering	0% New Model	0%	$ —	11. Align with regional contracting practices
80% Existing Customer			100% Existing Model	0%	$ —	12. Classic geographic expansion
		20% New Offering	0% New Model	0%	$ —	13. Transformational innovation
	100% Existing Geo		100% Existing Model	16.00%	$ 160,000	14. Existing customer product migration
		80% Existing Offering	0% New Model	0%	$ —	15. Offer new acquisition models
			100% Existing Model	64.00%	$ 640,000	16. "Milking the cow"
			Total	100%	$ 1,000,000.00	

$1,000,000 Growth Goal

FIGURE 6.2 Growth Framework Output: Fortune 500 Company

- At least 80% of revenue comes from existing customers.
- Within that existing customer base, 100% of revenues come from existing geographies.
- Within the existing geos, 80% of revenues come from existing products.
- Within those existing products, 100% of revenues come from existing business models.

If you expect that the remainder comes from "new," then the following is also true:

- 20% of revenue comes from new clients.
- 0% comes from new geos.
- 20% comes from new products.
- 0% comes from new business models.

Figure 6.2 shows how these results map to the model if we assign a $1 billion growth goal.

Our results show you get some interesting insight from the model based on our inputs. There are really only four pathways that you need to worry about. These four Growth Pathways – 16, 14, 8, and 6 – are the PRIME PATHWAYS. Prime pathways are the most used means of growth. Every company, without exception, uses these four pathways. Full stop. Start-ups, mature businesses. For-profit, not-for-profit. B2B, B2C. Regional to global.

Another way to look at the Fortune 500 example is that for our company, 12 of the 16 pathways are unlikely to be worth the investment. There is a huge value here as you avoid investments that could lead to a waste of effort or time. Knowing what NOT to do is invaluable as you think through your growth strategy.

Okay now let's consider the other end of the spectrum: a start-up. How would that look?

- Let's say we have a revenue goal of 3,000,000 over 5 years.
- Well, let's say that only 40% of business over the 5 years would come from existing customers (since we'd be working hard to get and keep new customers).

- 100% would come from an existing geo, since we wouldn't have the ability to expand right away.

- 50% would come from existing goods and services because we had planned new offerings as the business grows.

- 70% would come from existing business models, since we are going to offer new aaS capabilities.

This is really different from the large company picture (Figure 6.3).

- Pathways 6 and 8 are the largest, with each representing 21% of revenue.

- Pathways 14 and 16 are second tier with 14% each.

- Then there are four new pathways to consider – each with "new model" revenues – 5,7,13, and 15.

What's interesting about these (which we will see in later chapters) is that you access all four new pathways simultaneously simply by offering a new business model.

It's a simple decision tree, and like all decision trees, it provides the structure to frame a multivariate problem in an exhaustive, logical way. You make educated guesses at each fork about likely probability. Those educated guesses, when combined, provide analytical insight about the potential sources of revenue and their relative importance.

A few rules:

1. Each branch of the tree is assigned probability. The collective probability of nodes on that branch needs to total 100%.

2. Pathways are made up by connecting successive nodes to each other across the Four Key Questions.

3. The percentage of total revenue by pathway is calculated when each node percentage for that pathway is multiplied across the four questions to derive the probability of each scenario. In our example we would multiply 40% (Existing Customer) times 100%

Growth Framework Output

Created for **Startup**

Property of Cliff Farrah/The Beacon Group - not for distribution

Color coding represents relative attractiveness of each pathway.

The darker the revenue percentage and target revenues are, the better it is for you. Medium gray pathways require discussion. Optimal pathways are bolded.

Customer	Geography	Offering	Business Model	Percentage of Revenues per Pathway	Target Revenues per Pathway	Growth Pathways
		50% New Offering	30% New Model	0%	$ -	1. Pure innovation testbed
			70% Existing Model	0%	$ -	2. Offensive market disruption
	0% New Geo	50% Existing Offering	30% New Model	0%	$ -	3. Testbed for disruption
			70% Existing Model	0%	$ -	4. Geographic expansion
60% New Customer		50% New Offering	30% New Model	9%	$ 270,000	5. Innovation share grab
			70% Existing Model	21.00%	$ 630,000	6. Classic growth via product/service improvement
	100% Existing Geo	50% Existing Offering	30% New Model	9%	$ 270,000	7. Introduction of disruptive business model
			70% Existing Model	21.00%	$ 630,000	8. Classic new account addition
		50% New Offering	30% New Model	0%	$ -	9. Disruptive innovation
			70% Existing Model	0%	$ -	10. Regionally focused new product development
	0% New Geo	50% Existing Offering	30% New Model	0%	$ -	11. Align with regional contracting practices
			70% Existing Model	0%	$ -	12. Classic geographic expansion
40% Existing Customer		50% New Offering	30% New Model	6%	$ 180,000	13. Transformational innovation
			70% Existing Model	14.00%	$ 420,000	14. Existing customer product migration
	100% Existing Geo	50% Existing Offering	30% New Model	6%	$ 180,000	15. Offer new acquisition models
			70% Existing Model	14.00%	$ 420,000	16. "Milking the cow"
			Total	100%	$ 3,000,000.00	

$3,000,000 Growth Goal

NEW GROWTH

DEFEND AND GROW

FIGURE 6.3 Growth Framework Output: Start-up

(Existing Geography), times 50% (Existing Offerings) times 70% (Existing Business Model) to give us a value of 14%. That represents all revenues you will earn from Pathway 16: Milking the Cow. Since we set a target of $3 million for the 5 years, that means we can expect to sell $420,000 through this pathway in that time frame. You would do that math for each pathway to generate your result.

4. There are 16 potential pathways in the tree we have presented. This is designed to keep our planning process strategic and high level.

5. You have to consider aggregated behavior over the time frame being considered – that is, for a 5-year plan, what percentage will come from new versus existing across the Four Key Questions. We will break that down to annual forecast in later chapters.

Now take the answers you provided at the start of this chapter. Remember the "quick drill" I asked you to do? Put the % for each question on the existing branch and put the remaining % (100 minus the existing) into the new branch. Do this for each question, and you will have populated the framework. This should take about 5 minutes. Multiply each % out, and you will get percentage of revenues by pathway. That should take another 5 minutes. Multiply those percentages against the aggregate growth targets, and you will get a revenue number by pathway. This should take another 5 minutes. So in 15 minutes, you've been able to create a top-down 5-year revenue model for your company.

Take a moment and think about both how simple this is to do and the fact that you can do this exercise not only for your growth but also to assess what competitors are likely to do. In the defense world they would call this a "black hat" exercise; in the commercial world we might call this a game theory exercise. We will come back to the Growth Framework in later chapters, but you can see that it is a powerful way to think about a critical growth question – where will the money come from?

Notes

1. https://www.ctpost.com/business/article/Reports-Sikorsky-close-to-landing-2™ndash;1-billion-15082197.php,   https://www.nytimes.com/2014/03/07/business/international/worlds-biggest-arms-importer-india-wants-to-buy-local.html;   https://www.business-standard.com/article/companies/tata-sikorsky-jv-to-make-aerospace-components-109111300102_1.html;   http://www.defense-aerospace.com/article-view/release/109809/sikorsky.

2. https://thespoon.tech/dunkin-hints-at-its-future-with-self-service-kiosk-expansion/.

3. http://www.china.org.cn/english/BAT/94973.htm,   http://en.people.cn/200210/10/print20021010_104756.html.

4. https://www.computerworld.com/article/2504152/evernote-launches-china-based-note-taking-service.html,   http://www.oneskyapp.com/blog/how-evernote-reached-four-million-users-in-china-within-1-year/#:~:text=Evernote%20launched%20its%20localized%20service%20in%20China%20in%20May%202012.

7

The Process Overview: How to Build a Growth Strategy

Having a repeatable, structured, teachable process and a consistent, well-understood vocabulary as you talk about planning growth is critical. The best of the best can do this across business units consistently. Process matters.

Process and rigor have quite a bit to do with planning successful growth, especially if you are trying to get beyond being lucky enough to be in the right place at the right time with the right offering. There's always a luck factor that you cannot ignore, but corporations of scale need to be more than lucky; they need to be consistent. Our process leverages internal knowledge and external assessment to drive down risk and improve the likelihood of sustainable repeatable success.

Like a master chef, the ingredients, how they are introduced, and the cooking method combine with timing and temp to create a consistently fantastic dish. Successfully creating sustainable, scalable growth is very similar in its need for consistency of process.

This book presents both a framework and a process. We just did a quick review of the Growth Framework, and it's what I had the most fun creating. Based on my experience in growth strategy development, it's one of the most powerful ways to think through the different ways a company can grow. But it's a tool, and like any tool it needs to be used in a process. When building a home, a contractor always uses a table saw, but only to cut lumber to meet the needs that the architect identifies in the blueprint. Developing the blueprint is what our process enables.

Usually, you are either engaging in this exercise by yourself or as a part of a larger team. The process works in either situation, but we will be talking about using this approach as a team leader and will use callouts to identify areas that would be different if you were working on this by yourself.

In the services world, we have a saying: "Consistency equals quality." That means that one way to test the capability of a firm is to assess the consistency of process and evaluation across its spectrum. David Maister first wrote about this in the groundbreaking *MIT Sloan Management Review* article, "The One-Firm Firm," where he correctly made the point that it is critical to have a repeatable, commonly understood process to use across a services organization. As a growth strategist – whether an entrepreneur planning your future, or a manager in a large enterprise, or even a consultant advising your client – you are providing a service: the creation of growth strategy. So, as you consider growth planning every year you need to have a repeatable, known approach.

This lesson is well demonstrated when you consider the armed forces. I have had the privilege to know and work with Lieutenant General (LTG) Gene Blackwell almost since the founding of Beacon – first as a client and then as a core part of our Defense team. General Blackwell is one of the rarest of growth strategists who succeeded not only on the field of battle but also in the business world, and I am grateful to have had his steady hand on my shoulder throughout the evolution of our firm. A proud Clemson alumnus, LTG Blackwell served two tours in Vietnam; attended the Marine Command and Staff College and the Army War College; and served in the 82nd Airborne Division (where my dad served in World War Two), where his son served and his grandson serves today. He had infantry assignments at the company level in Vietnam, at the battalion level in Germany, at the brigade level at Fort Lewis, and at the division level at Fort Stewart. He served as the Assistant Division Commander for Maneuver in the 3rd Armored Division for Operation Desert Storm where he says, "I was responsible for the close fight, which was an unfair fight, but still a fight." Following his command of the 2nd Armored Division (Forward), he returned to the US to command the 24th Infantry Division (Mechanized) at Fort Stewart, Georgia, and then was assigned to the Pentagon as the Army DCSOPS (G3).

After that tour, he left the service to take a leadership role at Raytheon, where we met, and I served him as an advisor for many years. It's clear that he is well-versed in strategy development but also in command and execution across a massive force. He not only can plan but also he can successfully execute, which is a critical skill for success in growth strategy.

After he left Raytheon, I was able to convince him to join our team as a senior advisor, a role he continues to serve with distinction for our clients as they navigate the seam between the government and commercial world.

General Blackwell and I have had many conversations about the role of process in consistent execution, and he shared the role of process in military strategy.

> You need to know that from the very beginning, when people enter the military, one of the first things they are taught, and this is true for the Army and from Marine Corps to the Seabees . . . they are taught a five-paragraph order. It's called a Five Paragraph Op Order or Five Paragraph Field Order. It's a very simple process and what it's designed to do is to give a structured format that makes it easy to execute missions . . .

Think about the power of this statement for a second. Across the military branches, each leader has been taught how to think through and achieve mission success. They have a common language. A common thought process. A common toolkit. You cannot overvalue this as a strategist. This gives confidence, power of execution, efficiency, competence. Imagine the power this common knowledge and practice would provide if EVERY member of a company's leadership team operated the same way. This would eliminate so much misunderstanding and accompanying conflict, inefficiency, waste, and time lag.

I am a fundamental believer in this notion. You MUST have a standard approach and process, and I'm pleased to be able to offer that with this framework. This process is a blend of both success and failure. In legal terms, this process has quite a bit of negative know-how or prebaked avoidance of points of failure. I think of them as scars. If you follow this proven process, I think you'll find it's very effective.

Another reason this process is so important is that it leads to a much higher probability of effective execution of strategy.

Rob Hays is Vice President and Chief Strategy Officer for Lenovo Data Center Group. In this role, Rob leads market intelligence and strategy development for Lenovo DCG worldwide. Prior to his current role, Rob was Vice President and General Manager of Strategic Planning for Intel Data Center Group, where we got to know one another. Rob is an incredibly hard-working strategist and has created billions in value for the companies where he has worked. In his current role, he has over 6,000 employees in the organization he serves, and his decisions impact each of their lives.

I had a chance to talk with Rob about not only the challenge of coming up with the right growth strategy but also the hurdles of successful execution:

> There are a couple of handoffs as you go from strategy development to execute and go to market. There's one handoff where you've got a strategy team and an executive decision-maker or decision board that's going to kind of buy off on a strategy. That's Stage One. Stage Two is once you get it in execution. You hand it off to . . . different sort of functional leads [who] are going to execute to it. You can't have all those people involved en masse upfront, but you definitely need to have their expertise at the table. There's a third handoff or Third Stage, which is go to market and you're getting the sales team engaged.
>
> The thing that resonates with me is . . . you need to get buy-in for the follow-through. You'll buy a small tuck in acquisition because you think it's going to be the greatest thing to improve a product line. You buy them, you integrate them. You often lose some of the people [who] came over from the team and then you eventually give it to the sales team to go sell, and they're like: "I didn't want this!" If you didn't get the buy-in from sales sooner, it dies on the vine. You have to figure out how to get that kind of go-to-market buy-in upfront and that sponsorship all the way through."

FIGURE 7.1   Beacon's Growth Strategy Development Process

Rob is spot on. You have to make sure you are engaging the entire team throughout, and we will talk about that next. It's not enough to come up with a good idea. You have to convince people to get behind it, and our process is built to do that.

Like every effective process, it has to be clearly defined, easily understood, easily taught and replicated, and it needs "loops" to allow iterative development as new learnings are absorbed (Figure 7.1).

There are seven steps to the growth strategy development process I developed at Beacon to use with our clients.

1. **Define business objectives.** This step requires discipline, is typically very hard to do, and is often uncomfortable for leaders to create with their teams. To successfully define business objectives, you will need to be able to articulate financial, timing, and strategic objectives, socializing them with core team members and get them to understand the *why* of the targets. Do not underestimate the difficulty of defining business objectives well. Get this wrong and nothing else matters. This step is as much about the *why* as the *what*.

2. **Internal assessment.** In this step, we use a series of questions to understand the creature we're bringing to the fight. The internal assessment digs into a company's internal strengths and weaknesses to determine the most natural growth pathways to pursue.

3. **External assessment.** In this step, we determine both the terrain of the battlefield and the creatures we are up against. Both the customer landscape and competitive landscape are considered, so the growth strategies account for the current and future customer requirements and competitive pressures in a given market.

4. **Analyze and select growth pathways.** A team-based exercise, the Growth Framework is used to exhaustively consider all the potential ways a company can grow and then flunk as many as possible. This is where we apply financial objectives as a reality check with the team to determine the revenue value of each potential approach against the goals and objectives established in Step 1.

5. **Select strategies.** In this stage, we developed the underlying strategies and tactics to be used. Another team-based exercise, what's important about this phase is to harness the experience of core team members in an unfettered way as a baseline. Then their strategies are augmented with the inclusion of expected or traditional strategies associated with a particular pathway. Tactical planning questions of who, how, what, when, and where are also measurable actions with associated costs. This is critical as we enter the next step.

6. **Model returns.** Unlike typical strategy processes, our model is tied directly to financial goals and needed outcomes. This is highly unusual and prized by our clients as a practical way to drive investment decisions in growth with predictable returns for their business.

7. **Map strategy to a timeline.** Each strategy includes a number of pathways, and there may be synergies or challenges when combined.

As you pursue the development of a new growth strategy, it is extremely important that you exhaustively consider what you *could* do before you commit to what you *should* do. You should also be able to repeat this process over multiple years, and across the different areas of the business. In the services world, consistency is quality, and growth strategy development is a service.

Most companies we work with have some version of this process. The value of this framework and process is the standardization of approach, commonality of language and definition, and the ability to drive a consistent structure to consider different growth strategy across the business.

We will talk to each process step in subsequent chapters, but those steps are milestones on the journey. First, let's consider who will be on the adventure with you.

CHAPTER

8

Creating the Team

It's all about the team. Get the right team, and you'll do well. Get it wrong, and it won't matter how good the plan is. Sheri Dodd, whom we met in Chapter 5, is a vice president and general manager at Medtronic Medical Care Management Services, and she put it this way:

Sheri: It's funny, I think when I was chartered the first time to build a growth plan, I didn't have appreciation for what was really being asked of me. I thought I was being asked kind of to go do something individual. You know, go get some job done, and I figured that if I could just spend enough time thinking about it myself and organizing my thoughts, carving out, say, 40 hours or 80 hours, I could probably just go knock it out of the park.

Cliff: It doesn't work like that?

Sheri: It doesn't work like that.

Traditionally, strategy has been the domain of the chief strategy officer, product line GM, owner, and so on. "Ivory tower" strategy is a term that talks about how classically strategies developed by these roles in an ivory tower – the rarified air of the thinker – are then passed down to business units for execution.

This is simply a flawed approach, and unfortunately from the early days in my career I have the scars to prove it.

At Beacon, we ask that our clients staff each Growth Framework exercise with the representation from each functional area. At a minimum, we want to have the following organizations represented:

- Strategy
- Marketing
- Sales
- Ops
- R&D
- HR
- Finance
- Legal

One of the most accomplished strategists I know is Tom Lattin. Some people plan, some people do, very few excel at both. Tom is Vice President of Product Planning and Strategic Technologies at ZT Systems. I got to know Tom in his prior role at HPE (Hewlett Packard Enterprise), leading the ProLiant and Cloudline server product lines. Tom is an iconic figure at HPE, where for 26 years he held a variety of leadership roles. From servers to notebooks, PCs and cloud-focused offerings, Tom was the catalyst for billions of dollars of revenue growth in his career. I love his use of parable from our discussion about the importance of functional engagement.

> So, there's a glass of water sitting on the table and finance guy walks in and he's shaking his head. Says "Glass is half empty, right?" Then the marketing guy walks in. He's like, "Oh my gosh, look at that. That glass is half full, right?" And then the engineer, who's really kind of pragmatic realist and looking for everything to be efficient, says, "That glass is the wrong size."

[You need all] . . . three of those types . . . The one thing that I think important, regardless of whether you're Optimist, Pessimist, or Strategist kind of operational thinker is that you have a strong sense of empathy for other functional areas. Empathy for the customer. Empathy for other partners in the market – that would be part of your recipe. Whether they're distribution channel or technology partners/suppliers. Because having not only an understanding but a sense of the motivations, the opportunities in the fears of the care of all those players become very important. I think in the dialogue about what are you going to do right. [What are you] as an organization going to do in that context?

Still don't appreciate the importance of the breadth of the team? A few more leaders have shared their perspectives and explained it to me as well:

James Klein, President Infrastructure & Defense, Qorvo:

The best pitch, the most rational, market-based, competitive-based strategy that I ever did in my career, and I was incredibly proud of it, was a complete failure! The failure was because we underestimated the transformation it was going to take inside the company to go where we needed to go. I think we were perfectly right; it would have driven growth, and we would have done great. But we didn't understand how hard it was going to be for finance and operations and supply chain and engineering to go from point A to point B.

Dave Murashige, VP Offer Management, Aria Solutions:

I think you actually have to engage the entire top half of the organization, and by that, I mean your senior leader team has to all be on the same page. They have to understand what you're trying to do, and more importantly, really be committed to it. . . It can't just always be top-down autocratic kind of approach . . . there isn't a function that gets left out and there isn't a leadership level that gets left out. The top cadre of people have to be aligned and then you expect them to do that same alignment with their own teams. Every one of the major functions contribute to the success: HR, IT, finance, sales, marketing operations. You can't find an organization that doesn't have an integral part to play.

Nancy Callahan, Global Vice President Services Strategy, SAP:

> I definitely agree with your approach, and that you can't do it in an ivory tower . . . I think strategy does need to have both a longer horizon probably than the typical line manager and also some space to just think about things differently away from the pressures of day to day. Because you can't do both. Very few people can do both; you can manage teams to do both, but it's really hard for an individual to be in both modes of thinking. That's where you need to consult with the experts who are in those functional roles.

Mitch Mongell, CEO, Fort Walton Beach Medical Center:

> It's so important to involve those on the front line. As an example, I took over a hospital and found that we had a brand-new MRI. Open MRI was brand new, state-of-the-art, so why aren't we using it? Well, my predecessors never involved the radiologist. They were angry that they weren't involved and said, "I'm not using it." It was a million-and-a-half-dollar open MRI machine, but they didn't want that size, so they said, "we're not using it." You learn that you need to involve the end players to be sure that everyone is aligned on the same strategy.

This is a sample of the stories that I learned when we talked about the importance of inclusion when creating a strategy. There are too many great quotes to choose from. You can listen to each of the interviews available at Beacon's podcasts at www.beacongroupconsulting.com to hear more.

The Three Critical Groups

When you consider the functional areas listed previously in this chapter, you can break them down into three groups: the Thinkers, the Doers, and the Vetoers.

The Thinkers

The Thinkers are the traditional developers of strategy: GMs, Strategy, and Marketing roles. They live in the world of the big picture, and they have strategy as part of their job description. These are the folks who understand possible scenarios emerging and have a sense of how markets can be shaped. But while they can think it, they don't typically drive success. That must be grounded in the reality of the Doer.

The Doers

Doers are the ones who execute the strategy: Sales, R&D, Ops, HR. If they don't buy into the plan, you are wasting your time. Countless strategies have failed because the strategy was "pie in the sky" when rolled out to the staff. By engaging the Doers throughout the process, you ensure that you can consider and engineer out failure points.

Human Resources

HR is a non-obvious member of the strategy development team. But most growth strategy comes down to people. If the business is already at full capacity, you will have to add new resources. That takes time. Or you may have to retrain existing resources, which may not be possible given the mix of current employees and their skill sets. Only HR can give you guidance on that.

Research and Development (R&D)

R&D creates new products. You have to recognize engineers aren't just sitting around waiting for you to call on them. They are busy researching and developing last year's, or the prior year's, strategic focus areas and aren't resourced to take on something new. So, either they will ask you to give up a current program area of focus or they will ask for more budget and resource (which HR has to get for them!).

Operations

Operations determines what will be produced, by when. So, when you decide you want to launch a new product, they will be the ones determining production runs, supply chain, capacity planning, retooling, packaging, distribution, and any other requirements to support the rollout of a new product. Of course, they will highlight cost, trade-offs, and resourcing requirements. Ignore them at your peril!

Sales

Sales makes the magic happen. If you don't engage Sales, you don't sell. If you don't sell, you die. Sales drives cash; cash pays bills and generates profit. The challenge with Sales is that any change to the status quo is disruptive. New products and technology require training. Increased geographic coverage requires people. New business models require new comp plans. The Sales force at your company is a group of thoroughbreds. Executing well on the sales front requires up-front thought on the challenges you will face. Engaging Sales is critical.

The Doers allow you to identify and solve for the execution challenges your strategy will face. And what you will learn the hard way is that it is much better to successfully execute an effective strategy than it is to create a brilliant one that fails. Strive to be the most *effective* strategist, not the smartest one. You will have the most success this way.

The Vetoers

The most neglected and feared group are the strategy killers. I cannot count the number of strategies in my career that have made it to a final briefing only to be vetoed by Finance and Legal. Co-opt them early and make them part of the strategy and you will find clear sailing to the finish line.

> **PRO TIP**
>
> *Nancy Lyons Callahan*
> *Global Vice President, Services Strategy,*
> *SAP*
>
> I really do believe diverse perspectives matter and having both diversity of thought in terms of functional expertise like sales and those with "veto" power. I love that characterization of finance and legal.
>
> I think it's useful to have people who do have deep experience in the area that you're studying and those who don't, because you can get caught by your own past and it's hard to

break free from that sometimes. Or you fall into "Oh, we tried that two years ago. I'm not going there again." We are doing some things in terms of strategy that we tried five years ago, because my answer is you can be right and you can be right at the right time. Anybody who's been in business for a while has had those experiences whe[n] you are ahead of the market or ahead of your time. It happens all the time.

Finance

Finance worries about, well, financials: hurdle rates, return on investment (ROI), net present value (NPV), discounted cash flows (DCF), investor relations, resourcing. When strategy gets to finance, they will argue that a threshold won't be met. That there is no budget. That they can't in good conscience justify the investment of resources in the strategy. By engaging them early, allowing them to voice concerns as the strategy is modeled, you will preemptively deal with the veto. Let them build the financials. Let them defend the assumptions. You will find that you have much more success when you engage Finance early.

Legal

Legal is the risk mitigator. Legal reviews strategy with an eye toward exposure, existing contracts, and potential misstep. This is incredibly necessary, as is the Finance function. You cannot allow strategy to be created that risks what the company has built to date. Rather than waiting until the team is enthusiastic about a strategy that Legal views through a risk-based lens, engage them early and give the team runway to address the challenge. You will always be more successful if you understand and can address the concerns of the Legal team.

***

Thinkers, Doers, Vetoers: Each has their role to play in the creation of an executable growth strategy. When you leverage their experience, harness their knowledge, and engage their creative engine, you not only avoid pitfalls but also you can truly create an executable strategy.

One of the most amazing things about writing this book was how much I learned from the great leaders who contributed to it. I went to one of the world's best business schools to learn about effective leadership, and I am vain enough to think I am a good leader, but I am humbled when I talk with leaders from the military. I cannot fathom the depth of responsibility you must feel when you are committing soldiers to a potential death. The importance of team when considering life and death is incredibly clarifying and has so many valuable lessons for us all. Lieutenant General Gene Blackwell offered the following thoughts on leading a team:

> Successful teams, whether in the business world, or in the military, I believe, have to have a common focus. I think they have to have a clear, shared vision for what they're trying to accomplish, they have to have open communications, they have to prepare thoroughly as a team, and each member of the team has to know what their duties and responsibilities and limitations are so that they can execute accordingly. They must clearly understand the mission or expectations assigned to them. They must have the ability to adapt quickly. They must have a determination to succeed. There must be a recognition of success. And the team has got to feel appreciated. I think it's very important to do that and they have to believe in the leadership. You would think that would be more important in combat or in military operations, but it's just as important in industries or whatever; you got to believe that the leadership has the best interest of the organization and thus your best interest at heart.
>
> It's different in the military because you're committing people to a possible death, and so I think in the military you feel more associated with the people . . . when you stand in front of this group, some of them are going to die in very short order, and I've experienced that and it's a very humbling experience. But the other thing is there must be trust in the leadership. There must be a commitment to a common cause, and they must have a feeling that they can be heard.

If you are developing this strategy on your own, with no access or mandate to the leadership of these functional areas, you have to role-play from their mindset as much as possible to develop the executable strategy. Consider the challenge from the functional point of view of the Thinkers, the Doers, and the Vetoers.

Another key element for success is a team member who thinks and leads as an entrepreneur. A catalyst to keep the team together and high functioning when the task becomes difficult. It doesn't have to be the top dog, but you need people who won't quit when the going gets tough.

Marty Curran offered an interesting insight on the kinds of people who make the best entrepreneurial-minded scientists:

> We did an HR study: Why is it that some scientists are entrepreneurial, and others aren't? We learned that the ones who had to do something entrepreneurial in their younger days, paper routes, sold lemonade, did something like that where they interacted with people would be the ones [who] are more entrepreneurial.

He went on to talk about how important that is on a team and for a manager connecting personalities for success. While this is a simple learning, I believe there is a relationship to the kinds of people who are effective growth strategists.

I tested this theory across the entire group who participated as sources for this book, and they each had a great story. Athena Murphy painted a picture of herself as a young girl in a rainstorm throwing Sunday papers. Stories came from each person I interviewed. Neighborhood lemonade stands, working at the family business, babysitting, grass cutting, haying . . . each person I interviewed worked at a super-young age.

I asked Bryan Simms to participate in this book. Bryan is an intuitive leader; has led a successful career in financial services at Morgan Stanley, JP Morgan, Lehman Brothers, Lazard; and is now deep into life as an entrepreneur with Traffk, a software and services company where he fills the role of Chief Corporate Development Officer. He's been a great advisor to me throughout the years, and we are godparents to each other's children. I was talking with him about his role as catalyst and shared my theory. I wasn't surprised to learn his young life followed the same kind of trail. He started with a paper route. Then he was a bellhop. By his 18th birthday he had his first job thinking about growth with an iconic Boston brand: Steve's Ice Cream.

> There was a two-year period of time that I was out of school where I worked in a retail ice cream shop founded in Boston called Steve's Ice Cream.

Full disclosure, Steve's was the best of the best back in the day. Frankly, I couldn't get enough of it (as my high school yearbook photo shows). He went on:

> Durham, North Carolina, never had anything like that before. One of the biggest projects I was charged with was to figure out how to grow that business, and I had no idea, no training, no background, formally. It was all gut intuition, informed by experience and fear. The experience taught me to simply look at where we could sell our highest margin products and to figure out how to increase volume sales around them. I understood that math because it was taught to me by the two guys that I worked for, one of whom was a local businessman, the other one was soon to become the majority owner of the Boston Celtics.

I love this story, because like every other person interviewed it shows that no matter how successful you are, you started out as someone just trying to figure things out as best you could. We all do that every day as growth strategists and it goes to the importance of every member of the team. We get better at it for sure, but it's always the same challenge. I encourage you to embrace the notion that, if we are lucky, we are always learning. The other thing you often see is that someone took practitioners under their wing at a young age and showed them how things really worked. For me, it was my dad. He opened my eyes at a young age to how the world worked, and I've always appreciated that. I hope I've passed those lessons along to my children.

On Trusting Your Gut

Team members will make or break your success. As you get more comfortable with this process, you will recognize that we are providing as much of a change management process as we are a growth strategy development process. If you are able to engage with your team across functional areas, even the naysayers will become invested in the success of the strategy they helped build. It is a very powerful method to engage the strength of the entire organization.

However, you have to trust your gut.

There may be members of the team assigned to you whom you feel uncomfortable with. To be clear, I don't mean that you dislike them because they disagree with you – you don't want agreement. If everyone agreed with you, you would be better off making the strategy by yourself!

No, I'm talking about people you don't think are flexible enough in their thought to change their position as they learn. These people are poison. They will cause you to fail.

How do you recognize them? An inflexibility of position. A dysfunctional, argumentative attitude. An inability to be empathetic. The insecurity of something to prove. A lack of creativity. An unwillingness to argue against their own position. There are quite a few ways to determine this, but you will feel it. Initially you may not be able to define why you feel the recoil of engagement with these people, but if you are a leader, you need the people on your team to be reasonable and engaged, not opinionated and prideful.

These are people you want reassigned. I know that is a political landmine within a larger company. You will have to work with these people daily. They won't forget their removal from a team. So, it's very important that you preemptively engage with the functional leadership or business unit leadership to select your team members.

I am not encouraging you to select yes-men or yes-women. On the contrary, I'd rather have people who I know will argue every potential fail point with me. I don't want teammates who will make our job easy; I want teammates who will challenge my thinking. But, when I've considered their concerns, and the team has come up with a viable workaround, I want them to acknowledge it and get behind the plan.

Not everyone can do this, so it's important to trust your gut and engineer out the people who could lead you to disaster in this effort.

Necessary Grit

A marginal strategy with a great team will succeed.
A great strategy with a marginal team will not.

So, now that we have the team squared away, let's dive into the process.

But before we begin, a harsh truth: There is a critical success factor I cannot teach, and you won't learn it in this book – it either has been developed, or it has not, and it may never be. It is a factor that has either been taught to you at a young age, or an event forces you to learn later in life.

Simply put, it is force of will. Grit. The unrelenting doggedness and commitment to overcome hurdles, naysayers, and roadblocks. Whether a corporate player or an entrepreneur, if you have this stuff in your marrow, in your spirit, then this book will help channel it. It will teach you how to be more effective and efficient as you plot your course.

If, however, this is a new concept to you, that you believe in the fairness of process and lack the lessons about life that only failure can provide, then know that the odds of your success are lower. Growth is not easy to execute – you can work through to the "right" answer, but you will need to develop a new muscle, a new spirit, a new determination that you may not yet possess.

This is a tough thing to consider. Even without the lessons here, those who have the "will" to succeed actually do it. In my experience, more than 50% of failure comes from the wrong team in the wrong role. I've interviewed hundreds of corporate leaders to identify the critical attributes of success, and the number-one consistent theme is that at some point, you make a bet on the team. On the people. Those who will, do.

I've met and worked closely with quite a few warriors in my life. I count Seal Team members and Special Force operatives among my friends and colleagues. And then I've met corporate warriors, people I know who, like those in the military, worry about their teams before themselves. True corollaries to the operatives I know and how they think. They are committed and pragmatic. They are corporate citizens with the power to challenge their world for the betterment of the company. And usually, for me to like working with them, they are simply human, and aware of the personal challenges that growth strategy can present to teams. People who get this are like "rare earth elements". . . things that we can simply never get enough of to meet demand. Frank Soqui is one of these. Frank's North Star phrase is "coalition of the willing," which he uses to describe people working together to do what they know is right for the company instead of worrying just about power, position, or compensation. Frank is the real deal, willing to take a hit for the team and strong enough to speak about what he thinks is right and why. Frank currently serves as the Vice President and GM of Desktop/Workstation and Channel Group at Intel, where he's been employed across the company for 38 years. I've known and worked with him over the past decade, and I've never met his equal in strategic thought. Ignore this man at your own peril. I asked him to talk about the greatest challenge for a growth strategist.

> The challenge is the will to execute. That's what it really comes down to. Once you've gone through planning, you have to have the will to execute and it's not for the faint of heart. Sometimes you get bored and sometimes something doesn't go exactly the right way. You don't know how to pivot and enhance. But I'd say by and large these truths are self-evident. It comes down to the culture and the constituency of the leadership to go make these things happen.

From a distance, growth is achieved by a company – up close, it's guerrilla warfare, an intimate and personal challenge. My goal is to give you the weapons to win the fight.

CHAPTER

9

Defining Business Objectives

Step 1: Targeting the Hill We Need to Take

Setting business objectives seems like it should be the easiest part of the strategy development process. As a leader, setting and communicating the goals for the organization is a core part of the job and is easily and uniformly done, right? Unfortunately, this is rarely the case.

> It starts with what is the most important process or the most important statement in all of this; it's called *"The Commander's Intent."* This is what I intend to accomplish by this mission. Okay, we're going to go liberate Kuwait. That's what we're after at campaign level. But at a platoon level, it may be to attack the next hill and to occupy that hill.
>
> Lieutenant General Paul "Gene" Blackwell

Setting clear objectives isn't just important in growth strategy, it's important for any endeavor. The military teaches this across its branches as the most basic element of successful planning.

Rami Rahim is everything you would hope for in a CEO of a publicly traded company. He is smart, funny, humble, and perhaps most importantly, genuine. His strengths come through in the talent he attracts, the excellence he projects, and the loyalty he has for his company. Rami is the CEO of Juniper Networks, a California-based multinational company that serves the networking market with hardware, software, and service-based solutions. Generally accepted as a technology leader, Juniper's products are associated with best-in-class solutions, a position that is hard to establish, let alone maintain. Rami was employee number 32 at Juniper, which now has over 10,000 employees across the globe. An engineer by training, he has had a meteoric rise through the company to the role he now fills. Rami graciously made the time to share some of the journey he's had and the philosophies he has developed about how to successfully advance and execute on growth.

Rami talked about the importance of goals and their power in aligning an organization.

> Juniper, over the last few years in particular, has been on a transformation journey . . . and that touches on many different things . . . It's never easy to get leaders on board, or to get your broad population (in the case of Juniper, 10,000 people) on board with something like this. I really thought long and hard and studied this idea of creating a goals-based

culture and measuring ourselves against those goals. The system, the tools, and the processes were honestly quite secondary to that culture I wanted of excellence in execution.

Setting these goals and making them widely visible to anybody interested in seeing them has the effect of creating better alignment between people. Any leader can now orchestrate and define goals that align with the corporate objectives and also align with the goals of peers that are ultimately going to be part of the overall solution to any strategy or problem.

The other thing it promotes is improved accountability . . . you make it completely transparent to everybody . . . radical transparency can be a real gem. At the end of the day, I believe one of the most important ways to address and improve accountability is through peer pressure. If we all see each other's goals and we start to understand how we are all performing relative to those goals, any leader can ask probing questions and can put some pressure on teammates. I tend to go into our system and review how our goals are progressing on a regular basis and I can use that information to then ask the right questions to my organization. It really comes down to, especially when you're going through all this change, alignment, so we improve on execution and accountability.

Typically you find leaders who can give general direction or goals, but very few are like Rami and consider the Holy Trinity of strategy goals: financial, timing, and strategic. You need all three to succeed. The old saying is true: It's "ready, aim, fire," not "ready, fire, aim." The first step we have to take is defining the mission, the business objectives. Cleanly. Crisply. Unambiguously. Transparently.

Juniper is playing the long game, and its team understands that. It bodes well for their future success.

As a small company, an entrepreneur, you set these goals yourself. If you are a mid-sized company, owned by equity investors, goals are set for you by the investors. If you are a large-scale company, your goals are negotiated with your manager, and they need to align with the objectives of the corporation.

Don Scales gave an example for Investis Digital:

We're owned by private equity; you have your company goals dictated to a certain degree by your shareholders. They want to maximize their investments. So you start with what their expectations are, and then you start building off of that. So if you know they want to get out in 2 ½ years, and they want you to double in size, then that gives you some parameters to start working from.

Both Rami and Don give great examples of the importance of using goals to drive behavior. So let's shift to the ways we do that.

At a minimum, you need to define Financial, Timing, and Strategic objectives for your plan.

Financial Objectives

Businesses typically should have revenue goals and profitability goals. These are shockingly hard to pin down with senior leadership and getting sign-off on the objectives is a critical step for any team building a growth strategy. Revenue gives the baseline goal. Profitability goals help define how much you can spend to achieve the revenue. Some firms are focused on market share goals, which are fine but have to be carefully set.

When you set your goals, you have to make sure you are targeting the right thing and that you will be promoting the right behavior. Bob Roda, President and CEO of HemoSonics, has led quite a few planning exercises in his day, and loves what is referred to as BHAGs, or big hairy audacious goals.

The beauty of a BHAG is that it's a BHAG! And the danger of a BHAG is no one believes you can actually achieve it. We have an expectation as a business to outperform the market, to outperform our competitive set. What we don't always know is what's the ceiling? So we do point forecasts and pick a point in time and say, "This is where I want to be." The thing that I know as an economist is that the minute you write it on paper, it's wrong.

In financial goal setting, I try to define the appropriate amount of stretch that still makes it believable, achievable, and not punitive, because if we if we look at a market that's growing 3% to 5% and we say we want to grow at 20%, well everyone starts with a system of nonbelief. And so what are you actually getting? Generally, in those occasions, you're getting less than what you would have otherwise. This is a bit of art and science, and I like to describe it as the difference between baking and cooking. Baking is very prescriptive. There's a recipe. Chemistry. Cooking is about flavor and taste and too much of one overwhelms another, and so I think you need to understand how big you can be, and then you put some sense of realism as relates to growth and timing.

Bob went on to share an example of how financial goals, if not thought through, can cause the wrong behavior. He calls it stepping over dollars to pick up dimes.

> I was in a group setting and we were talking about rewards and recognition. This is going to sound odd. I asked, "Who gets rewarded more highly? The person who promises 3% growth and delivers 5%? Or the person who promises 20% and delivers 18%?" Literally almost everyone in the room said, well, of course, the person who delivered 5% and had promised 3%. Then there was this really cathartic moment when someone said, "But the other person delivered 18% growth!" This is stepping over dollars to pick up dimes, and happens when we create an urgency, perhaps around at times the wrong outcomes. And we reward and recognize those outcomes, and then we step back later and say what the heck happened, and in hindsight we did most of this to ourselves.

He is spot on, and I've made these mistakes myself in my career, and sometimes at my company. You have to take the time to ensure that the goals and rewards you set are distributed correctly to each part of the organization and ultimately to each of its members.

Revenues are the most obvious targets for us. After all, we are growth strategists, right? Revenues are literally the top line and depending on the size of your company are worthy of consideration. Some firms set goals based on a growth rate. That is, in year-over-year growth, they set a target for the company. Typically growth goals are set by a corporate objective. If privately held, you can set your own targets. If a publicly traded company, you will likely find yourself either trying to beat analyst expectations or at least on par for your industry.

One of the sharpest knives in any drawer is Pat Burns. Pat has this great blend of strategy knowledge, financial acumen, practical experience, and a good dose of humor. He not only sees the big picture; he sees the way to make things succeed. A West Point and Kellogg graduate, Pat currently serves as the COO of Gibraltar Industries. I've known and worked with Pat for many years in his prior roles as SVP Strategy for Dover Corporation and as VP Corporate Strategy at Johnson Controls. Pat also served as VP GM at Danaher Corporation, VP Marketing at Trex Company, Director of Corporate Strategy at DuPont, GM at

AOX, and he cut his strategy teeth in the General Management Development Program at Owens Corning. I'm a fan of Pat and his experience and work ethic. I appreciated his making time to discuss his thoughts on goal setting:

> The goals have got to be breakthrough . . . sufficiently above market that it's going to force the team to do things, not just one thing, but many things differently. Whether it's innovation, geographic expansion, acquisition to adjacent markets – they've got think beyond their current sandbox view. The number has to force people to get into new areas and do things differently.
>   Specifically, the metrics would be a revenue number and an operating margin number.

On revenue goal setting, ever heard of the law of small numbers? This law says that with small numbers, big growth rates are easy. That is if you sell $100,000/year, and you want to achieve 20% growth, you only have to sell $120,000 the year, or an extra $20,000. Seems reasonable. But if you are in the Fortune 100, and you run a $10 billion line of business, you would have to sell $12 billion, or an additional $2 billion dollars to maintain that growth rate. That is pretty tough to do and forces a whole different set of strategies into the mix.

Whatever the revenue goal is, make sure you think it is reasonable and communicate the *why* of the goal to your team. Revenues are going to be the burden that your sales team has to carry. Make sure they understand the logic behind the lift.

Profitability is the second goal we set. Revenue without an eye toward sustainable profitability is a false target. You need to worry about the profit equation:

$$Profit = Revenue - Cost$$

If the cost exceeds the revenue, then you lose money. That is not a sustainable construct. By setting a profitability or ROI goal, we can provide guidance on how much we can spend to get the extra revenue. And you will have to spend to get it. Whether it's more salespeople, new products, or new geographies that you will enter, you will spend it to make it. The key is to know what the ROI will be. In larger companies that will be defined as a hurdle rate or weighted average cost of capital (WACC). In smaller companies it will be more about keeping the lights on and everyone making a living.

All financial goals need to not be snapshots, but assigned with an eye toward timing objectives.

Timing Objectives

Financial goals need to be set with 2-, 3- and 5-year objectives. This is strategy, not tactics. Time horizons extend longer but should still be grounded with milestones to achieve the longer-term goal. By setting 2-, 3- and 5-year goals for revenue and profitability, we can consider growth rates and reasonable expectations in driving toward profitability metrics. Pat went on to talk about the need for time-driven goals:

> I really believe in what I learned at Danaher . . . You want to be 50% of the way there year one. That's where you set your objective. And as unreasonable as that sounds, it is really a smart thing to do because it forces the team to deal with the hard things first rather than push them off to the years 3, 4, and 5, right? You deal with the structural things first . . . Growth strategy suggests something longer term than the next 12 months. So forget year 1. Years 2 and 3 will be tough, but necessary, so that the plan doesn't show a magical "hockey stick" of growth in year 5. Year 5 guides the scale of the growth and determines quite a bit about what you set for years 2 and 3.

Rob Hays talked about the difference in time horizons he focused on during his time at Intel versus his current role at Lenovo:

> At Intel we had a very long view on everything because you had a 2-plus-year development cycle, you had a 3-plus-year process, and you had a relative life span of anywhere from 2- to 5-plus years per product. So you're looking at a 7-year horizon. It's such a big expenditure up front in R&D expense and capital expense that you have to look at it over a long period or you would just never do anything because it would never pay off in the first 2 or 3 years. You know at a company like Lenovo we have a much shorter time frame . . . we like to have things that pay off in the given in the current year, and we're not really looking at anything that doesn't pay off within 2 or 2½ years.

We will come back to the timing objectives as we move forward into the actual planning exercise, but know that growth planning looks beyond the near term; at a minimum a 5-year time frame is considered best in class, but can depend on your industry.

Value Rules of Engagement

Every company has a shared value system. Don Scales coauthored the book *How to Lead a Values-Based Professional Services Firm,* which is focused on teaching how to use values to manage a professional services firm. The stronger the value system of a company, the cleaner and more obvious the rules of engagement, or how you will compete in the market. He shared:

> Well, I think everybody has to understand what your value sets are. Because as you grow it's easy to deviate or stray from what your company values are . . . So people have to know what you stand for and what's important to you. Once everybody understands that and it permeates the culture . . . then I think you do a lot better job of being focused on your planning because everybody knows you're going to keep it within the bounds.

Some companies are extremely conservative and set boundaries in terms of marketing messages. Others use financial rules to enforce/embrace their values. Many talk about what people stand for. The bottom line is that values determine behavior, and understanding natural and unnatural behavior as you consider the development of strategy is key. Mitch Mongell talked about how much he strives to create a culture that embraces perfection – zero mistakes. He illustrates how important this concept is in the world of healthcare:

> You can't value what our product is compared to so many others, right? When you look at failures, a hospital needs to be 100% accurate. Because if I was 99% accurate, I would fail nine babies per year. When you put it in that context, if I was 95% accurate all the time then I would fail six hearts. When you think of it that way, there is very, very, very little room for failure.

Strategic Objectives

There are many strategic objectives a company may have. Strategic objectives are oftentimes driven by structure, values, philosophies, and other things that have little to do with day-to-day profitability and much to do with the culture of a company. They are strategic aims that need to be factored in as you think about how best to develop growth strategies.

Rob Hays at Lenovo offered this as an example:

> We're in a geopolitically charged environment, right? There's a lot of stuff going on with the trade war and the US saying, "China does this" and China saying, "The US does that" and it is causing a lot of supply chains to start to fracture for tariff avoidance and you know secure and controlled and all these reasons, right? And as a company . . . working for a company that has dual headquarters in the US and China, that affects us, right? And so we feel very strongly that we are an international company. We're a multinational company that does have dual headquarters that is not controlled or affiliated with any government entity anywhere, and so that is something that steers us.

He went on to give an example of how that manifests in their strategy:

> We are number one in supercomputing . . . one in three supercomputers run on Lenovo around the world, but we don't go after defense and nuclear. That's fine for others. There are other companies that specialize in that. That's not what we want to be known for, so we go after research institutes, universities, companies that are doing simulation, weather modeling. We think those benefit society.

We will consistently come back to linking the goals to the evaluation of the pathways. By defining this well up front, it is really easy to align and justify the investment and effort in generating the return.

Let's look at a totally different kind of strategic objective. I've been fortunate to know some great entrepreneurs. One of my favorites is a serial entrepreneur whom I met at Darden named Graham Anthony. I love Graham. His family. His work ethos. His transparency. His intent in life. I called Graham up, told him I was writing this book, and asked him to share the entrepreneur's perspective. On goal setting Graham offered the following:

> Being a [self-funded] entrepreneur gives you more degrees of freedom because you are spending your own money and you can take bets that you wouldn't necessarily take on behalf of someone else because you might want to be more of a conservator of their wealth. The times I've gotten in trouble actually are when I've been too conservative, too concerned, and people are saying, "I'm betting with this money; don't worry about it," and I'm like, "I worry about it every day!" So the nice thing about being an entrepreneur with your own money is that you can take bets and you know you only have to answer to one person.

He's right, of course. The challenge that you face as a self-funded entrepreneur setting goals is that, well, you are self-funded! Only you can decide what you want to achieve and how much you will risk for how long to get it. This is a terrifying, exhilarating, amorphous exercise. When you set a BHAG as an entrepreneur and hit it, you are incredibly successful. When you miss, you lose your house. For most people, this is high-stakes poker, and you have to be a realist as you consider what you can do with resources you have. But as I set out on my own 20 years ago – having just survived 9/11 by canceling my flight from Boston to LA – in a market that was in free-fall, with a pregnant wife and a 1-year-old child . . . there is nothing as satisfying as achieving and surpassing what you hoped you could do.

One of the things you get when you consider growth from the unfettered view of an entrepreneur is an appreciation of like/dislike. For example, I really, really dislike managing the cost side of client business. It's a very lucrative thing to do in my world, helping clients cut cost . . . I'm good at it and did really well at A.T. Kearney performing that kind of analysis. But as a person, I believe it carves away at your soul. Cutting cost to drive shareholder return eventually comes down to laying people off. I don't want to make my living that way, so – as an entrepreneur – I don't! Graham offers his own wisdom on this key component of setting your goals:

First, what are you good at? What do you enjoy? Michael Gerber wrote, "The purpose of a business is to give you more life." And he's talking about from the entrepreneur perspective. The purpose of the business is to give you more life. And I think if you go in every day to your job and say the purpose of my working in this job is to give me more life, then you're going to give more "life" to everything you do. Obviously, it would be tough for an English major to go into the lab and create something special. But to the extent that you have the skill set in that environment and the intent and have passion for and joy in what you set out to do, your work will be fulfilling and you're going to be more successful at it. So I would say, first and foremost, align your life and your work life in that way. Second, be honest with yourself. Get away from frustration by shifting your focus from what should be to what is. I think if we look at the world right today, there's a whole lot of *shoulds* that we'd like the world to be. But then there's a whole lot of the way it is. What is the reality on the ground? We have to navigate reality as we seek our goals. My mom would call it the serenity prayer, which if I recall is, "Lord, give me the strength to change the things I can. The humility to accept the things I can't, and the wisdom to know the difference." Something along those lines, and I think that's a really great bit of advice for us all.

Being an entrepreneur allows you the freedom to chart your own course, and your goals should reflect that. Remember why you took the risk to be on your own and set goals that will fulfill you.

Ultimately, though, your goals need to reflect both the top and bottom line. Tom Lattin says it best:

You know, many times we joke, "What are we trying to do with the business . . . is it about top line or is it the bottom line?"
And the answer is always, "Yes!"

If we've done this step in the process right, we have a clear set of business objectives to drive our efforts. Let's go on to the next step: the internal assessment.

CHAPTER

10

Internal Assessment

Step 2: Understanding the Force and Resourcing We Bring to the Fight

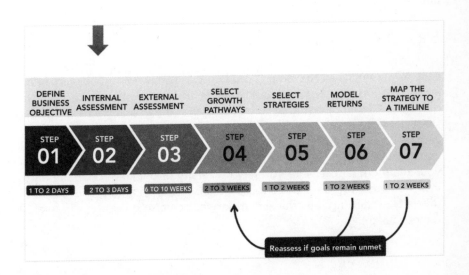

DEFINE BUSINESS OBJECTIVE	INTERNAL ASSESSMENT	EXTERNAL ASSESSMENT	SELECT GROWTH PATHWAYS	SELECT STRATEGIES	MODEL RETURNS	MAP THE STRATEGY TO A TIMELINE
STEP 01	STEP 02	STEP 03	STEP 04	STEP 05	STEP 06	STEP 07
1 TO 2 DAYS	2 TO 3 DAYS	6 TO 10 WEEKS	2 TO 3 WEEKS	1 TO 2 WEEKS	1 TO 2 WEEKS	1 TO 2 WEEKS

Reassess if goals remain unmet

In creating any strategy you have to be self-aware: who you are, what you are trying to do, your inherent strengths and weaknesses, and how you are resourced. I asked Pat Burns how important this step and the accuracy of this assessment was. Here is his answer to the question, "How accurate does this assessment need to be?"

> Well, near perfect. You've seen it too many times, as I have. You can have a beautiful strategy, but that's just a PowerPoint deck, right? You have to have a team that can bring that strategy to life and put in an operating cadence to go execute. If even one function isn't able to perform their needed role, it can keep you from executing well . . . You have to think about the team's bandwidth. Whether it has the ability to integrate or to manage a new product launch in a new acquisition.
>
> Here's an example. Our solar business did some very good market work. Good strategy work to figure out the tracker segment in their market. It is a great place to play, and they did a great micro market analysis and figured out where the attractive niche to play would be, where the big guys weren't. So, we started with an organic strategy. Concept was great, the design was good. But we didn't have the internal engineering capability and design process we needed. So, we launched the product. It wasn't ready for prime time, didn't perform in the field. We had to do a lot of remediation and it was just a huge black eye and was a big miss. We didn't have the product development, the engineering, really, the process steps put in place to make sure we had that design fully tested before we brought it to market.

Bob Roda gets the importance of self-awareness, too:

> I say to my teams all the time, "You know at some point dinosaurs had a pretty good gig. But as I look outside today, I don't see too many dinosaurs." I don't mean that to be sarcastic. I mean that we're in a constant state of evolution, so it's critical to bring collective insights together with an openness to listen, and to create an environment that allows for constructive challenge. The other part that's really important as you build your team out is to ensure you have diversity of thinking. Diversity and inclusion are a big deal and should be a big deal in all that we do, but diversity of thinking is a critical component because groupthink is a very dangerous thing.

Who You Are

When I first started to explain my process to staff, I used quite a bit of Darwinian language. What kind of animal or creature were we? How did we naturally exist/fight? What was comfortable versus evolutionary for us?

One of the reasons I love having Doug Fletcher as a board member is his true passion for professional services. He lives, eats, and breathes excellence in the services world as a daily goal. When we talked about understanding the creature you are, he talked about how self-awareness links to greatness.

What do you enjoy doing? You mentioned that and it's not intuitive. A lot of people say, well, why is that relevant? Well, the reason I think it's relevant is because it's hard to be expert at something in the services business if you don't enjoy it, right? If you're reading trade journals at 11:00 o'clock at night because it's fun or reading books on the weekend because it's fun, it doesn't seem like work, right? I think having a narrowly defined niche like Beacon is one of the smart things you've done since almost day one. You have said Beacon will be a growth strategy consulting firm and you've stuck to that. You have said no to other opportunities.

Companies are creatures. They behave organically in ways that align with a number of variables that are measurable. Show me a 100,000-employee company versus a 10-employee company and I will list a number of behaviors that are extremely likely. In a 100,000-person company there is strength in process, finance, continuity, diversification, footprint, product portfolio, history, brand, and culture. In a 10-person company there is creativity, aggressiveness, teamwork, transparency, speed, and flexibility.

It is incredibly important to know who you are. Too many times I've worked with companies or divisions of companies that have a very high self-opinion, who are ultimately small potatoes in a market versus competitors. I recall one kickoff meeting with a group that represented over $1 billion in revenues. And they were proud of that fact . . . until

I reminded them that they competed against companies that were doing $10 to $20 billion in their markets.

At the same time, I can list dozens of clients who don't recognize their strength in the market or massive elephants, timid about upsetting the ecosystem they exist in. Essentially these are companies playing not to fail versus playing to win. They were essentially asymmetrically held captive by smaller partners and competitors.

The goal of this phase in the process is to objectively assess who you are; your natural behaviors, strengths, and weaknesses; and the resourcing you have available to you. These answers determine the most natural pathways for you to pursue.

In warfighter parlance, we want to know the following:

- The force we have
- Its capability
- Its arsenal

In your role as a growth strategist, you probably have a good sense of the answers to this at a high level, but unlike efforts where we are studying competitors, you should be able to get a highly

PRO TIP

James Klein
President, Infrastructure and Defense Systems, Qorvo, Inc.

There are really only two things you can control. You can pretend that you control a lot, but there are really only two things. One, you can control who works for you and [who] doesn't. The other thing you control is the strategy of the organization so you can make sure that you set the long-term focus of where the group's going to go. So you know you've only got two things to do right. It's a relatively simple job; you just have to control who works for you and doesn't and where the groups are headed, and everything else will fall into place.

granular look at internal resourcing by functional area. Remember the team you have working with you. Each one can give you insight into their current state of capability: the health of the product portfolio, the staff you have available to help drive growth, the product pipeline that is in development. You need to leverage them all to understand in detail the capabilities and resourcing you are bringing to the fight. If you are an entrepreneur, you can likely answer all these questions without asking anyone.

Consider these basic questions:

- What are my values?
- How old am I?
- How big am I?
- What is my culture like?
- How much budget will I have to use in achieving growth?
- By functional area (Sales, Business Development, R&D, Operations, Human Resources, Finance, Legal), do I have additional headcount that I can count on, or will recruiting have to be factored into my plan?
- Are there any things we are doing now by functional area that are sacred and cannot be changed?
- How big and well protected is my intellectual property (IP) library/ portfolio?
- What are prior initiatives that are expected to mature during my planning period? How much revenue is expected from those efforts?
- How open are we to inorganic growth?
- What are boundaries for changes to our existing business model?

Answers to these questions are critically important for later stages of our effort.

Why? Well, one of the great frustrations of growth planning is having a great idea that cannot be executed.

Sheri Dodd offered the following thought:

A lot of time is spent thinking about strategy with this hope that with a really good strategy, the funding will automatically follow. Flawed approach. Part of setting this strategy is actually understanding how you are going to position it for funding. You can't just show up with a clear and compelling strategy and get support for funding. Building in the linkages and ties to the multiple decision-makers that either influence or specially approve large funding decisions whether it is directing new money, giving you EBITDA relief, or directing you to go back and find money within your AOP [annual operating plan]. All three are actually part of strategy development and I did not fully appreciate that. I feel like I've learned that late in my 25-plus years of experience. Even when you make the math work, to get strategy operationalized it takes money, explicit and intentional stakeholder management, and courage.

This is brilliant stuff that cuts to the heart of the matter. First you need the resourcing to win the battle, then you need the will. I couldn't agree more.

Pursuing growth usually involves people, and it's important to know if there will be dedicated resources focused on your plan, or if you are going to retask existing or hire new people to help you execute. As you work to develop strategies later, you will have to think through the importance of staff in each functional area. Need a new product designed? R&D headcount. Need to develop a sophisticated consumption-based business model? Finance.

Building growth strategies usually involves factoring in last year's plan. Unless you are a start-up, someone did this exercise before, and your company will be in the throes of executing on that plan. That means new products, penetration of new geographies, acquisition of new customers.

Kevin Watters shared how this works in the banking industry:

You've got these tranches from the years before that hopefully are starting to pay off, right? So you're doing a backwards look that says, hey, last year and the year before that, here are the things we said we were going to do. How are they now starting to play out? In banking, if you open a new branch, it might take 5 years for that branch to be profitable.

These initiatives have to be considered as you think through how to achieve your new goals. If they have expected payback in your planning window, you'll want to factor those in. If they have been earmarked as protected, you'll have to plan around them for resourcing. Knowing what your historic plan has been is critical as you think about your growth strategy.

What Are Your Corporate Values?

Values-based leadership, while considered a hot topic right now, is a time-tested critical factor for longevity and success in markets served. Values have power, real power. If you can articulate your values and defend them in your company, then you have perhaps the most significant variable to consider as you think about what you will or will not do in pursuit of your goals.

There are many examples, both positive and negative, that illustrate the impact of values. Frank Soqui talked about one of the tech sector greats, Craig Barrett.

Frank: There's an example we use from the Craig Barrett days, something called the creosote bush. It meant the thing (like a company's core product) that make it hard for other things to equal or rival.

Cliff: The creosote bush . . . is that what he called it?

Frank: Yes, the creosote bush. What a creosote bush does is it drops a tar-like substance from its branches to poison the ground around it, which starves anything else trying to grow up. Companies can behave that way. The CPU has been Intel's creosote bush. Everything else pales in comparison to investment in the ROI market segment share position, end in end, and we tend to measure other things as either stealing from that or can't compete with that kind of aspiration. And if you can't meet that aspiration, why are we even in it in the first place? Those are the dangers of being a big company and trying to decide you need to expand beyond your version of the creosote bush. Further, I believe that it applies in the personal and professional decisions that you make.

There is a wisdom in this that you have to consider through your own lens. If you think about your day-to-day, the things that are the core of your business, what are the sacred cows? The things that in a million years you wouldn't question about your investment and value in the market. The stronger you feel the emotion of protection, the more likely that is your creosote bush.

Rick Waldron has a résumé and background that make the most accomplished strategists stop and sit up straight. I remember the day I met Rick. In the services world, there are always clients who test you – they make you climb the mountain. It's a test – can you keep up? Can you lead? Do you understand their world? Can you connect disparate datapoints in a valuable way? Rick could, and somehow on that day I was able to keep up with him.

Why is Rick such an impressive strategist? Let's start with his education. Princeton undergrad, Harvard juris doctorate. Check. Check. Okay . . . what about work experience? Booz Allen as a consultant, stint in private banking, Intel Corporation at Intel Capital, and then lead of New Business Initiatives, VP Strategy and Innovation Accelerator at Nike and VP Strategy and Innovation at Mobe. Check, check, check.

What's hard to believe is how humble and appreciative Rick is as he approaches life. In a world where there's quite a bit of entitlement, I've never felt that vibe from Rick. He has unfailingly been interested in what I think. Reality is, he's interested in what everyone thinks, so I shouldn't feel special, but he has that gift to make you feel valued, which has enabled him to achieve such success. When I think about people who have a strong sense of their values, Rick is in the top handful, and you can see that as he talks about his current employer, MOBE.

We are a small 250-person company, and we are privately funded, which is an amazing gift. We are funded by a high-net-worth individual who started Mobe as a garage project in a large pharmaceutical company that he and his family owned. When they got out of that business, he continued to make investments in the health space. His vision was to fundamentally change the healthcare industry and to support people in achieving better health and more happiness. He looks at those things as inextricably linked, and he wants to address both without adding any cost to the healthcare system. So MOBE has a super-interesting business model where we basically take risk on a population of folks who are having a bunch of chronic conditions that they suffer from and who are high-volume users of low-cost health services. Five percent of the population drives 20% of the cost in a health plan. We serve these folks through what I will call deep empathy. We have coaches, "guides" we call them, who are health coaches. They have backgrounds as nurses, chiropractors, naturopathic, other things. They are deeply grounded in how to help people get healthier and happier. We are focused on empowering our users to take better control of their health and to break through. Our users have seen a bunch of doctors, they're on a bunch of meds, but there's a missing piece and they usually get Band-Aids on existing symptoms . . . not dealing with root cause issues. So we try to help them through better self-management to live a better and healthier life. We have proven results of lowering of healthcare usage and costs by a significant percentage because those people are getting healthier. I just sat through a town hall where we had one of our participants join and it brings tears to your eyes every time. These people have lived super-challenging lives. The fact that we can help these people live happier and healthier lives is just amazing to see.

In many ways, as I listened to Rick talk and reflect on the years I had known him, through the many incarnations of his role as a strategist, I was struck by the authenticity of his statements. This was a practitioner at the top of his craft who had found a role where he was proud of his company and the value they provided to the world. Knowing your value system, and what you would and would not do to achieve your aims, is critical if you want to succeed as a growth strategist. It's rare to find the clarity that Rick enjoys in his role, so I have to celebrate it.

Can You Pursue Inorganic Growth?

One question that always comes up as companies scale is the notion of inorganic growth, or growth through acquisition. This is an action that requires corporate commitment across the board, but it has many benefits if you can afford it. Knowing if you have access to the resources to buy other companies is critical as you think about achieving your aims.

How Flexible Is Your Business Model?

Finally, you should be very clear about whether or not you will be able to flex the business models used in your company. Companies who are aggressive and flexible on the business model have had huge success over the past decade, carving out share and even putting more inflexible competitors out of business. In particular, the move from large individual product sales to monthly payment streams has been a powerful tool for companies like Google, Microsoft, HPE, and Lenovo.

As you think through each of these attributes, you'll create a strong sense of self-awareness and what natural ways to compete will be.

I think it's time to introduce you to one of my board members, Hunter Reichert. Hunter has been on my board for over a decade and has seen us grapple with our own growth challenges. I don't say this lightly, but I've always thought of Hunter as one of the smartest people I know. His analytic capability, his capacity for numbers, his ability to connect numbers and people have made him invaluable to me over the years.

PRO TIP

J. Hunter Reichert
Founding Partner, Mangrove Equity Partners; Adjunct Faculty Darden Graduate School of Business, UVA; Board Member, The Beacon Group

Make a decision. You're never going to be 100% sure. If you're looking into change, whether it's a growth initiative, growth-focused initiative, or a person-oriented initiative. Make your decision.

We see a lot of companies and a lot of people, and a lot of leaders [who] are crippled by a lack of ability to make a decision.

Hunter is in the world of private equity. When you hear these words, understand that you are talking about companies that invest in, or purchase controlling interests in, other companies. Venture capitalists, equity investors – they have a million names. Hunter is a managing partner with Mangrove Equity Partners, where he is a member of its investment committee. Prior to cofounding Mangrove, Hunter was a founding partner of Harren Equity Partners. He's also an adjunct professor at the Darden School at UVA, where he teaches one course a semester on top of his busy work schedule. Now Hunter is what's known as an active investor. That means he buys companies with the intent to actively engage with their management to help them grow. He invests in what is known as the lower middle market, or companies that make less than $50 million a year in revenue. I've introduced you to him to illustrate the level of self-awareness that the best of the best strategists has. Here's what I mean:

> I think our place in the evolutionary process of a company is from that 20 (million) to 50 (million), or 20 (million) to 100 (million). We've had companies that have grown at that scale. When it gets to 100 (million), generally, we're not the right owner for that business. There's a better owner for that business and that better owner may be a larger fund, it may be a different company that has greater resources. We are very good at the blocking, tackling, facilitating, and supporting earlier life growth. Putting systems in place, putting processes in place, putting people in place. Once that is all done, we're generally transitioning ownership to a better group . . . a group that's just better configured to go from that 100 million to a billion dollars.

This is an amazingly powerful self-assessment. Hunter knows the sweet spot where his value starts to diminish, and I applaud him for being able to articulate it. Too many times companies miss their profitable exit. For Hunter, in his world of private equity, the notion of a better owner is not only humble, it's likely correct. The muscle and capability you need to have to create a billion-dollar business is very, very rare. Knowing your limits is critical as you chart your strategy path.

Knowing your company, it's culture, ethical and operational boundaries, and available resourcing allows us to plan for the battle ahead.

So, Step 2 complete – thanks to our internal assessment – and we now know the goal, the army we have, and how well we are resourced for the fight. It's now time for Step 3, the external assessment.

11

External Assessment

Step 3: Understanding the Terrain We Will Fight On and the Foes We Will Face

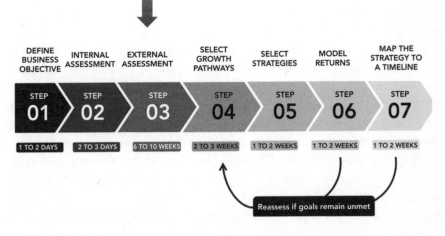

DEFINE BUSINESS OBJECTIVE	INTERNAL ASSESSMENT	EXTERNAL ASSESSMENT	SELECT GROWTH PATHWAYS	SELECT STRATEGIES	MODEL RETURNS	MAP THE STRATEGY TO A TIMELINE
STEP 01	STEP 02	STEP 03	STEP 04	STEP 05	STEP 06	STEP 07
1 TO 2 DAYS	2 TO 3 DAYS	6 TO 10 WEEKS	2 TO 3 WEEKS	1 TO 2 WEEKS	1 TO 2 WEEKS	1 TO 2 WEEKS

Reassess if goals remain unmet

In this step, we determine both the terrain of the battlefield and the creatures we are up against. The PECC (political, economic, customer, and competitor) landscape is considered, so the growth strategies account for the current and future customer requirements and competitive pressures in a given market.

Pat Burns, Gibraltar's Chief Operating Officer:

> This is really important. You want to have significant secular trends, macro trends that will give you above-GDP growth just by showing up. It's a heck of a lot easier for a team to grow and expand profitability in a growing market. If you are fighting volatility, cyclicality, headwinds, it's just 10 times worse, so we look for markets where ideally everything is in the control of our team.
>
> You want to minimize the external factors on outcome. You want to avoid volatility. One avoids cyclicality. Knowing ourselves, being self-aware, we avoid markets with rapid technology cycles, because we're not good at that. So, we want to play in markets where technology cycles are long, and we can see them coming and then we can grind our 1 ½ market times market performance without getting blindsided. So, there are a number of attributes that we look at market consolidation, in structure, more consolidated market. Rational competition is a better place to play, right?

The external assessment is the next step in our process. In this phase, we are studying the external world. PECC are all factors we must consider. Simply put, this is the terrain the battle will be fought on and the armies we will fight against.

This is not easy stuff at the most basic of times, and the pandemic has made it even worse! Pick a layer of an external PECC market assessment. Political? We just lived through one of the most divisive elections in American history. Economic? Well, unless the pandemic resolves quickly there will be significant uncertainty in the markets we all work in. Customers? Who knows what customers want right now because we haven't been able to talk with them the way we used to. Competitors? What metric shows how well your foes are braving the storm that is COVID? Unusual, unpredictable behaviors are the new normal. This is simply not easy to navigate. Oftentimes in the businesses we acquire there really isn't a product development strategy and a product development plan. There's really not a go-to-market plan. In many cases you would be shocked, but some of the senior members of management teams don't really have a full sense of what their market is, right? They know what their market has always been and that market has always served them well, but they don't know what their market can be.

If you want to get beyond being lucky once, being in the right place at the right time with the right offering, you have to constantly study the market to identify opportunities and threats, and you need to maintain that understanding over time. As the old saying goes, luck is when opportunity meets preparation.

Political Factors

It's hard sometimes to remember that businesses compete within rules entirely established by politicians. And that when these rules interact with employers and other countries, we get economic behaviors. Do you compete in an industry that is highly regulated? Does that regulation come from the federal, state, or local level? If you live in Europe, is it an EU or country regulation? When you cross borders, are there trade restrictions that you have to consider?

Marijuana is a great example. Legal at the state and local level of many parts of the US, it's still illegal federally, which precludes deposits to any bank that wants to be recognized as FDIC insured. This creates a tremendous number of hurdles for anyone wanting to participate in this ecosystem, including the storing of cash and the accepting of large cash payments for equipment (from growers who cannot deposit funds). Pat Burns talked about his holdings in this domain.

> You also want to avoid markets that are driven by regulation. We are in both marijuana and renewable energy and both of those are very much dependent upon regulation. . . it can cause unpredictability in the market. I've seen the solar market boom and crash three times in my career. And we're going through another cycle up because of investment tax credit issues.
> You want to avoid uncertainty and that's what we're being hit with in the marijuana market right now. The uncertainty around financing is causing capital to dry up in a growing market. There's going to be a whiplash coming our way once that gets sorted out.

Oftentimes when I bring up political analysis, people get wrapped up in the consideration of their own political party and the behaviors that party expects they will show. That has no place in this process. Period. Be a capitalist, not a politician as you go through this. You have to dispassionately consider the ramifications of current and likely future policy as you think through implications of risk, success, opportunity for your business.

Economic Factors

These include an evaluation the economic health of your ecosystem. Variables like growth in Gross Domestic Product (GDP), Consumer Price Index (CPI), unemployment, and exchange rates are basic considerations for any analysis. They collectively define the relative health of ecosystems we will be competing in. Each of these should be considered with an eye toward potential implications as you consider your plan. Is money easy to raise? Can I find good employees easily? Is my currency going to cause more or less attractive export opportunities?

These are macroeconomic factors. We also have micro factors to consider: local code officials, education and unemployment rates, regional and local economic variables, access to employees and their relative economic health.

Example: In the past year, under the Trump administration, US and China trade relations caused massive disruption to supply chains as the countries were embroiled in a bitter trade dispute. Right and wrong doesn't matter in an analysis like this – you have to be pragmatic and fact based regardless of your political persuasion. Ask yourself: Does this matter to me? Do I need to adjust my plan to account for this? Making sure you understand the real impact of both political and economic concerns will be critical to developing a successful growth plan.

Customer Analysis

Customers buy. They are the lifeblood of every business.
Without a customer, your business doesn't exist.

Soak that up for a second . . . all revenue comes from customers. Full stop. So, if all revenue comes from customers, then it's in your best interest to really know and understand their wants, needs, and behaviors.

You also need to focus on the markets with the most and best customers. If you take someone who is a great fisher and bring them to a pond with no fish, they won't catch anything. If you take someone poor at fishing, but bring them to a stocked pond, they will catch lots of fish. Markets and customers served are the same way.

You need to know everything you legally and ethically can about customers as you build and manage your relationships and growth strategy. There are a couple of key variables we recommend you study at market, segment, and account level.

Customer Acquisition Models – or How Clients Buy

B2B versus B2C versus B2G, big versus small, product versus services – customer acquisition models vary.

Over the past decade, customers have had more options on how to acquire goods and services. Some customers buy centrally, some through channels, some through subscription. Major differences exist as you work through customer segmentation questions. Government, enterprise, and consumer are all different buyer environments, as are large versus small. Toss in global markets, differences by geography, and the notions of behavioral segmentation, and you can quickly find yourself overwhelmed. Take a breath and worry about a few simple things:

- Do they buy systems or products?
- Do they buy directly or through channels/distributors?
- Do they buy products outright, or are they subscription/performance based?

Customer Current and Future Requirements

As hockey great Wayne Gretzky said, "I skate to where the puck is going to be, not where it has been." Understanding both the current and future landscape of the customer is critical. Customers are moving away from product and more toward solution-focused buying. This is true across industries, consumer groups, and government markets. What this means is that people want to buy a solution that was created for them and their specific challenge. This requires unprecedented awareness from vendors, and a willingness to create solutions that are more specific to use case, by vertical, by customer. Understanding where customers are going, the problems they are trying to solve, and how they will acquire those solutions is a critical time spend in our process.

Understanding how markets are changing, early enough to take advantage of that shift, requires an immense amount of focus.

Being a change agent is immensely difficult in a large organization. You have to define a future vision that is compelling to your company's leaders and the general staff. You have to convince clients to let you change how you serve them. You have to make massive, existential bets that are fraught with risk. It takes a unique individual to want to be tested this way and an even rarer one to fill the role more than once. Tom Lantzsch is one such man. Self-made, Tom started his career at working at Texas Instruments. He then joined Motorola, where he worked for 13 years, leaving to found and sell three companies before joining ARM where he worked for 10 years as their Executive Vice President of Strategy. In his current role he is the Senior Vice President and GM of the Internet of Things Group at Intel Corporation. Through-out an amazing career traveling the world with his family, he's driven success in his own way, always seeing patterns in markets and anticipating the development of new sectors. Tom is smart, driven, funny, and competitive. When he is not cycling with some of the best the sport has to offer, he is again serving as a change agent, leading efforts to reposition Intel for the future. Tom made himself available to talk about his philosophies on growth strategy, and he offered real wisdom as we talked about how to understand changing markets.

You know, 3 ½ years ago when I joined Intel the conventional wisdom was that data [sic] was going to get created by these sensors, and [sic] it was going to get transported in some way, and then all this application activity was going to happen in the cloud. When I looked at this space, again nonconventional wisdom at the time, I thought that all these applications are going to need data to move from the cloud . . . closer to where the data [sic] was created. That was the hypothesis I had, and I thought Intel was uniquely positioned to serve this future.

PRO TIP

Tom Lantzsch
SVP Internet of Things Group, Intel Corporation

If you've got a great idea, don't blab about it until you need to, and get out ahead as far as you can. Because timing is everything.

If you are in the tech world, you understand that he's talking about the Internet of Things (IoT). In the original thinking of what the IoT would look like, Tom is right: We all had a vision of low-power sensors, sometimes even stickers that you could slap on motors, or in rooms or on doors, to monitor and control simple functionality. But, as the markets continued to emerge, new use cases started to emerge that were less passive monitoring and more active environmental management. Faster, more-complex decision-making that couldn't rely on a cloud environment.

Sorry, I went a bit nerdy there . . . we've all watched Netflix, right? When you are in the thick of a movie and it locks up on you, that's annoying. Now imagine your self-driving car has the same problem because the steering application runs in the cloud, not in your car. If you lost signal, or for some reason couldn't connect . . . well, that's not good. Tom could see this was coming and he stepped in again to lead the company toward his vision. He went on:

No one was talking about it. I certainly wasn't talking about it, because I didn't want to; the downside of being in a big company is they don't move as fast as you want, so just shut up and do your thing so that when the race starts you're ahead of your competition. So even if they are faster you are a couple laps ahead of them on the track.

Tom not only figured out a significant opportunity to lead but also he knew they needed to figure out the specific use case that would drive this change in behavior:

What was the killer app that was going to drive people to change? We thought connecting cameras and providing vision systems to cameras was a horizontal capability that was going to cut across every vertical I served. It didn't matter if it is a manufacturing plant where you'd use those cameras to do quality inspection, or we've got customers like Audi that inspects five million welds a day on cars. Doing that speed and doing high quality, that was a big challenge they had that we could solve. Or it could be, in a COVID world, replacing barcodes and doing cashless transactions at retail spaces. One of the things you may not know about barcodes. Theft is pretty high on self-checkout when you only use barcode. People scan one item and then put something else in the bag. Pretty common, but if you combine a camera watching the transaction with the barcode you can do detection of the object. So we thought that video was the killer catalyst. The challenge is you were creating so much data you couldn't send it to the cloud economically even if you wanted to, and you couldn't act upon it quick enough!

Bottom line: Tom thinks that the way we are built to handle information today just doesn't line up with the needs of that future state. Forget the technical jargon if it's not familiar to you. Assume he's right; I for one believe that he is, and I've studied the hell out of this question. The point he's making is that he saw an inevitable shift in the market coming that he wanted to lead.

Sailors know all about this; we are constantly looking up a course to see how the wind is shifting to be in better position than our competitors when the shift hits. Tom had such vision, such commitment to this idea he literally joined the one company he thought could lead the way and has spent the last 4 years of his life getting the company ready for that pivot. It's impressive stuff. Gretzky would be proud.

How do you learn about the market? There are quite a few ways. Hiring a firm like Beacon is one. We are incredibly good at understanding the current and likely future landscape of the market. But you don't always have to hire a consultant. You generally do that when you can't figure things out for yourself.

I really like how James Klein pursues understanding the market. As you consider this approach, know that there are examples from almost every leader I interviewed for this book who talked about how they get close to their customers.

If you don't understand what your customers really need, then you don't understand the market. So I think you've got to get out. My personal way . . . I spent lots of time on the road with customers. I also like to pick "favorite customers" and it's not favorite because they're the biggest revenue necessarily, or because they are the nicest to me, or because we get the best quality scores. They're favorite to me because I think they're customers that represent market trends. You know, maybe they're at the forefront of where a certain market is going. And so I like to pay particularly close attention to those kinds of customers because I think it helps judge how you're doing. If you can win with them, you can win anywhere. And so I think it's really important to pay attention to customers.

One of the great things about customers is that, if you are brave enough, you can talk to them. Now they will know they are talking to you directly, and that will likely bias what they share, but you can listen to them directly and, if you are savvy enough, figure out what they are looking for.

On Customers and Products That Never Existed Before

Once you get past the challenge of understanding how to listen to your customers, especially if you are a visionary thinker, you run smack into the reality that customers don't always know what they want!

There has been a lot written about this topic. How do you introduce new products to the market that have never existed before? How can you estimate demand for something no one has ever bought?

Nancy Lyons Callahan is someone I've gotten to know over the past year, and she's proven to be someone with serious strategy skills. In her current role as Global Vice President of Services Strategy, she sets the course for the behavior of SAP's 20,000 worldwide service employees. She's had an amazing career, as President of Reuters Futures Services, establishing the GLOBEX platform across exchanges in Chicago, New York, Bermuda, London, Paris, Frankfurt, Tokyo, Hong Kong, and Singapore. She led AIG's commercial, financial, and professional liability divisions. She served as Chief of Staff to the President and COO of Concur and is incredibly active with her beloved UVA, where she received a bachelor's degree in systems engineering and an MBA in finance.

I was delighted when Nancy agreed to share her thinking on strategy development, and we got into a nuanced discussion on this very topic of how you listen to customers about things they don't yet know about. She framed the challenge well:

> You do have to have the external view, which is both market scanning and then the customer view. There's always this tension that we need to be sure that we're serving the needs of our customers, but our customers don't always have the answers, either . . . Sometimes the greatest ideas do come from just being there side by side with your customers. But they have their own set of blinders. You need to survey the [market] landscape and look for analogies in other industries and identify what are the disrupters that even our customers have not anticipated. That is some of the fun of strategy.

She's spot on in both her assessment of the challenge and her approach to solve for it. When you are introducing a new technology or product to the market, you have to either look at success in other industries for the same product or focus on the functional capability of your offering. What does it do functionally that people do today? How do they consume that function today? What do they pay for that capability? Is current performance lacking? Would a substitute be welcomed? When you have discussions about functional capability, then you get past the distraction of cool or complex technology to the meat of why they should be sustainable.

Knowing your customer, their current and future wants and needs, the opportunity to offer them something new and transformative, and how they like to procure goods and services is perhaps the most important step in our market-facing process.

At this point, we should pause and consider progress on our journey. We know the goal, we know the army we are taking to the fight, its capability, and its arsenal. We know the terrain we are on (political/economic realities) and the value of what we are fighting for (customers). Now we need to focus our efforts on understanding the armies we are up against: our competitors.

Competitor Assessment

Once you've studied your customer, you need to understand the force you are up against. Your competitors.

James Klein at Qorvo offered his thoughts on understanding the competitive landscape:

> It's really important to pay attention to where your competitors are going, not where they are today. It's irrelevant where they are today, right? It's what are they likely to do when you do whatever you're going to do? That's very, very important.

There are corollaries between the internal assessment and the competitor assessment. The biggest difference is simply that you aren't an insider. Legally you are precluded from having insight into areas a company deems proprietary. So, you are limited to studying them from data visible in the public domain. The good news is that this task is doable if you are smart. You can plan a campaign to face off against the foes you face.

There are many measurable variables that are consistent ways to assume the capabilities and likely behavior of a company. *These are rules that work for any industry and any company.*

- **History/age.** Older companies have more rigid cultures and resistance to change despite best efforts to the contrary. As the scale of operations staff grows to support growth, process rigor is inevitable. Process = rules, rules = resistance to change.

- **Headcount.** A corollary to history/age, companies with larger headcount act differently than smaller companies. Hierarchy, process, systems, investment savvy, predictability, financial heft all come with headcount.

- **Revenue.** Larger companies (think revenues in the tens of billions) are generally publicly traded (not always true, but mostly). That introduces shareholders, investor relations, and highly regulated behaviors. It also generally has an established brand, a broad customer base, and is likely international. Smaller companies (think < $10 million in revenues) are typically privately held, incredibly flexible in behavior, and typically try new and disruptive things to differentiate and enter existing markets. They will likely practice organic growth and are a potential acquisition candidate.

- **Growth rate.** This is undervalued in most assessments in my opinion. Fast-growing companies like to maintain their rate of growth. The larger they are, the harder this is to sustain (law of large numbers). Pay attention to the company and division performance over time, as well as any stated goals you can find in the public domain.

PRO TIP

Tom Lattin
VP Product Planning and Strategic Technologies, ZT Systems

Even at a scale of $10 billion or more, I have to believe there's somebody actively working on growth strategies to completely disrupt the position I have. And therefore, I need an engine aimed at self-disrupting my position and that engine absolutely has to be focused on growth.

Even smaller entrepreneurial companies need to maintain growth rates to sustain staff and careers for employees. What is not obvious is that a targeted growth rate can drive quite a bit of unnatural behavior as companies look for new ways to achieve goals. These behaviors can require a significant response from competitors. Acquisition, new product development, geographic expansion, business model shifts all become transformative evolutions achieved to sustain growth rate.

- **Profitability.** The double-edged sword. Profitable companies are stronger companies and have more options financially. At the same time, higher levels of profit limit the number of attractive market opportunities for companies that have set investor expectations to meet or exceed a particular standard of return. Companies tend to avoid non-accretive investment opportunities – especially if they are larger/more sophisticated businesses.
- **Market share.** Playing not to lose or playing vs win. That's the mindset you should have as you consider your competitors. If they are dominant, they will be defensive. If you are dominant, they will attack.

- **Geographic footprint.** Companies that compete globally behave differently than companies that are "local." Know the portfolio of players you are up against.

- **Product portfolio.** We have clients who have thousands of engineers building products and a legacy of technology and IP that has never been introduced to market. Big product portfolios and IP libraries allow larger companies to leverage prior investment.

- **Access to investment dollars.** Is the company acquisitive? Do they have a history of growing through M&A? Will they likely use that as they work to meet growth goals? This would require a strong understanding of potential targets and their relative value.

- **Available operating assets.** How much armament does each competitor have? Are they out of bullets or do they have an arsenal ready to bring to the fight? In a COVID world, you have to consider the unpredictable nature of impact to competitors' resourcing. You have to know the likely strength of your opponent.

As you finish considering these different competitor attributes, you will have completed gathering all of the information necessary to build a world-class growth strategy. You now know the following:

1. The goal
2. The team you are taking to the fight and the resourcing it has to fight with
3. The landscape you are fighting on
4. The armies you are up against

Ask any strategist, and those are the things that let you lay out a good plan. Time to work on the fun stuff now – applying the Growth Framework.

CHAPTER

12

Select Growth Pathways

Step 4: Decide Which Route to Take

Situational awareness is a term used in the military. It's sort of the warfighter equivalent of emotional IQ. For growth strategy development you can meet savants of strategy, people who have the immediate understanding of a situation and the right path to take to achieve goals. In the military it might be battlefield awareness, where a commander in theatre can see the path to victory. While this is a great skill to possess, you can use the Four Key Questions to come to the same intuitive conclusions that an experienced strategist would reach.

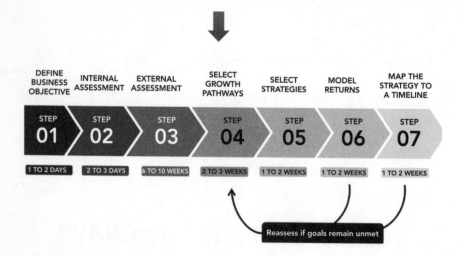

Imagine yourself on a battlefield. You have a goal – the mission. We defined that in the first step of our process. You look over your shoulder and see your troops. They are in formation, or in disarray. They are armed with machine guns or with rocks. The veterans are quiet in disciplined preparation, and the newbies laughing nervously as they face their first battle. Then you look forward. The ground is barren and flat, or it is urban and filled with pedestrians. It's dry and warm, or cold and covered in snow. In the distance, you can see the foe. It is a large army, or a rag tag band of fighters. They are beautifully arrayed, or in tatters. They have missiles, or spears. You know how they have fought battles before . . . And they stand between you and your objective.

This is the battle you will face.

This isn't hyperbole. Strategy is both a game of intelligence and also a game of risk. The employees of your company will count on you to choose the right path forward, and if you choose wrong, some could lose their jobs, their homes, even their health. You have to acknowledge the stakes to be great at this.

So, how do you approach thinking through all of the ways to achieve your objective? How do you know that you are exhaustively considering the universe of ways you could grow?

These are pretty typical and overwhelming questions for a new practitioner of growth strategy development.

Let's talk about the way you use the framework in a large group planning exercise.

Step 1: Pre-distribute the Four Key Questions Worksheet

In an email, 1 week before the planning session, send the team the Four Key Questions and have them return it to you. It is a simple drill that asks about the percentages of revenues for each key question, broken out by existing versus new. Ask them to take no more than 10 minutes to fill it out and return it to you. This is meant to be an intuitive exercise. This will serve as the basis for our top-down analysis. It's important you send it at least a week early so that they can forget about their responses as we go into the deeper off-site planning session.

This first step gets to the biggest challenge for a growth strategist – getting to the 30,000-foot level. For junior or senior staff who haven't been asked to think this way, forcing this kind of a thought process will be really powerful. We want this to be a simple, quick drill on their part. Don't discuss the goal in financial terms, just ask, to achieve the goal, how much revenue will come from existing customers? How much revenue from existing geos? How much revenue from existing goods and services? How much revenue from existing business models? Collect the worksheets and consolidate the data. Bound the percentages by question with high and low values and try to note who the outliers were by name.

Step 2: Bottom-Up Growth Framework Drill

As the first activity in the growth planning off-site (or virtual meeting) walk the team through the 16 Growth Pathways. Email or distribute hardcopies of the worksheet (found on our website at www.beacon groupconsulting.com or www.growthetopline.com) and use it to discuss how the framework is constructed and what each pathway means.

This worksheet is simply an unpopulated growth framework that team members will work through, and it should help structure the dialogue.

The next step is to walk the team through your efforts to date. Remind the team what the goals are that were defined in Phase 1. Show them what was generated in the Phase 2 self-assessment. Distribute and have them review the Phase 3 information developed during your PECC assessment.

Now turn to the tool. Encourage each participant to consider each pathway from their own personal/functional perspectives.

Drill 1 – On the worksheet they should check the box of every relevant pathway they think the company is either doing today, or should pursue to achieve target revenue goals.

Drill 2 – Next to each check mark, have them write down the percentage of revenue each pathway will generate. Make this point clear – this is what the team will commit to each pathway generating, and it cannot be fluffy. Ask them to imagine that their compensation was tied to that number, that their bonus depended on the numbers generated. It has to be that hard hitting and real.

This is where a bit of the art of the practitioner comes in. You need to get agreement from the group on what the values assigned to each pathway should be. The values of "new" and "existing" branches by node need to total 100% for the tool to work correctly.

If you are leading a group in this exercise, you aren't only trying to get to the "right" answer; you are trying to teach a common thought process, you are working to create a cohesive team, you are working to change how the organization thinks and behaves. For your strategy to be executable, this part of the exercise is critical to do well and requires some skill in facilitation. If you are doing this by yourself, well, you have an easier task, except you have to force yourself to consider the problem from the views of the functional leaders as you draft your numbers.

We want this team to struggle at this point. Struggle to learn a new framework that will feel uncomfortable at first. Struggle to understand why they believe what they believe. Struggle to listen to other opinions. And finally struggle with how much they are willing to commit to the go-forward plan.

Which are the no-brainer pathways? Which ones are absolute flunks? Of the remainder, facilitate a discussion about which ones make the most sense to invest in and what kind of return you will expect in the planning time frame. Once you get the group to consensus on this, make sure you capture exactly the chosen pathways and the amount of revenue, growth, or profit that you would expect to see from that leg.

Step 3: Share the Results

Gather the worksheets from each participant and collate the results.

- **Top down.** Use the Four Key Question drill to populate each person's Growth Framework by assigning percentages to each branch of the tree and multiplying out to get total revenues per pathway.
- **Bottom up.** Use the scores you got the group to agree to to populate the framework. Multiply the growth goal (total dollars) by the summary percentages by pathway to get the revenues per pathway.

As a group:

- Analyze and discuss the variance between top down and bottom up across the team.

Our goal here is to demonstrate a few things to the group:

1. Quite a few of the ways you could theoretically grow *aren't practical and should be killed.*
2. You can get to your goal with "traditional" or "natural" pathways that reflect ongoing business practices, not extraordinary means.
3. There are likely some good "evolutionary bets" to make in some of the risky buckets that should be considered and funded as the company looks to the future.

Let this discussion range and breathe. We want to encourage a consideration of all opposing viewpoints here. This could take the better part of an afternoon or an afternoon and morning session the following day. This is where art and experience come in, and consultants are usually a great value add.

At the end of this session, you should have a model that all functional leaders understand and sign off on. This book isn't on change management or facilitation techniques, but it's important that you get this step right.

There's a lot of classic change management and consulting theory embedded in this approach that you certainly don't have to do to generate a strategy. However, I think you'll find this is a pretty efficient way to get the team engaged and (at the end of it) bought into the output.

Figure 12.1 shows what the top-down Four Key Questions output would look like if we had a growth goal of $2 billion at a typical Fortune 50 client.

Model assumptions are 80% existing client, 100% existing geo, 80% existing product, and 100% existing business model.

By building a decision tree from the Four Key Questions with the "new" branch for each question being the remaining percentage to reach 100%, you can build the same output as the bottom-up exercise the team went through. It's a simple exercise and has great power.

I like color-coding the results. Red is almost always something you'll avoid investing in unless you are making a long-term, high-risk bet. Solid green is a must-do. Figure 12.1 shows this grayscaled; see the legend.

Figure 12.2 shows another way of looking at this.

Let's take a second and think about the output we've got.

The good news – there is almost nothing unnatural about getting to the goal. It involves tried-and-true practices. It leverages customer trust, generates revenue from existing portfolios, stays relevant through the sale of new goods and services, and uses business model approaches that are understood both internally and externally.

Of the 16 ways this company could potentially grow, they really only have to worry about four, the prime pathways we discussed in Chapter 6. This analysis shows that 64% of our revenues will come from basically doing what we already do: existing customer, existing geo, existing offering, existing model = Pathway 16: Milking the Cow. In this example

Growth Framework Output

Created for [Typical Fortune 50]

Property of Cliff Farrah/The Beacon Group - not for distribution

Color coding represents relative attractiveness of each pathway.

The darker the revenue percentage and target revenues are, the better it is for you. Medium gray pathways require discussion. Optimal pathways are bolded.

Customer	Geography	Offering	Business Model	Percentage of Revenues per Pathway	Target Revenues per Pathway	Growth Pathways
			New Model 0%	0%	$ -	1. Pure innovation testbed
			Existing Model 100%	0%	$ -	2. Offensive market disruption
			New Model 0%	0%	$ -	3. Testbed for disruption
			Existing Model 100%	0%	$ -	4. Geographic expansion
			New Model 0%	0%	$ -	5. Innovation share grab
			Existing Model 100%	4.00%	$ 80,000,000	6. Classic growth via product/service improvement
			New Model 0%	0%	$ -	7. Introduction of disruptive business model
			Existing Model 100%	16.00%	$ 320,000,000	8. Classic new account addition
			New Model 0%	0%	$ -	9. Disruptive innovation
			Existing Model 100%	0%	$ -	10. Regionally focused new product development
			New Model 0%	0%	$ -	11. Align with regional contracting practices
			Existing Model 100%	0%	$ -	12. Classic geographic expansion
			New Model 0%	0%	$ -	13. Transformational innovation
			Existing Model 100%	16.00%	$ 320,000,000	14. Existing customer product migration
			New Model 0%	0%	$ -	15. Offer new acquisition models
			Existing Model 100%	64.00%	$ 1,280,000,000	16. "Milking the cow"
			Total	100%	$ 2,000,000,000.00	

ATTACK AND GROW

20% New Customer — New Geo 0% — New Offering 20% / Existing Offering 80% — New Model 0% / Existing Model 100%
Existing Geo 100% — New Offering 20% / Existing Offering 80% — New Model 0% / Existing Model 100%

$2,000,000,000 Growth Goal

DEFEND AND GROW

80% Existing Customer — New Geo 0% — New Offering 20% / Existing Offering 80% — New Model 0% / Existing Model 100%
Existing Geo 100% — New Offering 20% / Existing Offering 80% — New Model 0% / Existing Model 100%

FIGURE 12.1 Growth Framework Output

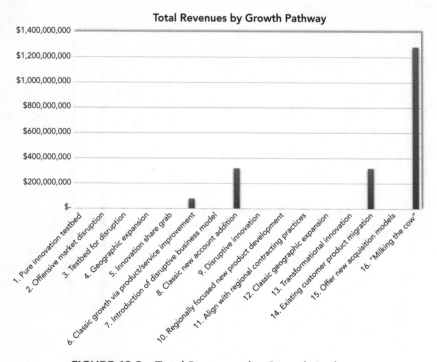

FIGURE 12.2 Total Revenues by Growth Pathway

that's worth $1.28 billion in revenues for this client. As Elvis would say, this is just normal TCB.

Subsequently, you can see only three other pathways that are viable colors. Pathway 14 is Existing Customer Product Migration, or "selling your customers something new," and Pathway 8 is Classic New Account Addition, or "hunting down a new customer." Both are absolutely normal and natural ways for companies of scale to compete. Our model says that each one is worth about 16% of our goal, or $320 million, while Pathway 6: Classic Growth via Product/Service Improvement is going to drive about 4% of goal, or $80 million in sales.

So, you can see the might of the top-down approach. Four simple questions, intuitively answered, that lay out the foundation of our plan for growth.

This particular model example is what I use to teach about how large companies compete. When left to their own devices, this is what the heavyweights do, and they are really, really good at it.

Our example company's focus on these four prime Growth Pathways is also their Achilles heel. They ignore other pathways because they don't have the associated revenues that big companies need to see to get excited. More on what this means in Chapter 13.

Let's talk about questions that will definitely come up with people once they start to wrestle with the tool.

How Do I Define "New"?

For each group it varies, but it has a lot to do with intention. A new customer is someone you have to work through the entire sales process – awareness, interest, consideration, procurement – all steps that new customers go through. Existing customers are already aware of you; they already have trust and have transacted with you, which can be a big deal depending on your business. You have to intend to get a new customer to justify new expenditures in the strategies and tactics that it will take to capture them. New geo is literally revenue generated and transacted from a geography you don't currently serve. Intent plays a big role in this one. If you intend to generate a lot of revenue from a new geography, then you'd typically have to invest in footprint there. It's one thing to just put a rep in a new country, it's another thing to open an office. But revenues from new geographies would be contracted there. New offerings are pretty obvious from a build standpoint, but not always when you think about selling a customer something new. The reason this is a Key Question has much more to do with the risk of development of new goods and services and less to do with selling an existing product to someone who hasn't bought it before. If you have to build something new, it belongs in "new." If you are just selling something you've already built – it goes in "existing." Last but not least is business model. This is how you sell your goods and services. If you've always sold your product but are now moving to a leasing model, that would be "new." If you have always sold through a distributor, but now are going direct, that would be "new." Generally, changes to business model, as we've discussed, are a really big deal and are typically either an attack mechanism for smaller companies or a defensive play by larger companies forced to respond to the changing market.

If I'm Starting a New Company, Wouldn't Everything Be "New" and Go through Pathway 1?

Excellent question, and I think the answer is no. When you are actually building your company, you know what you are going to offer right out of the gates. Before you open your doors, you have defined the kind of creature you are and what your "natural" behaviors and pathways will be. Therefore everything would fall under Pathway 8: Classic New Account Addition. That said, you are running the process, so if you want to treat start-up revenues as Pathway 1: Innovation Test Bed, that's fine for year 1. After that, everything would shift down to Pathway 8.

If We Are Planning over a 5-Year Period, Would Something "New" We Do in Year 1 Become Existing in Year 2?

This is a great question, and the answer is yes. If you acquire a new customer in year 1, they become an existing customer in year 2. If you develop a new product in year 3, it becomes an existing product in year 4. There are two ways to account for this in your planning process. Either you can run five different models and aggregate them, or you can allocate by year or by pathway. I prefer this method, and it looks something like Figure 12.3, which uses the example of the Fortune 50 plan we discussed previously.

In this case, as you can see in Growth Pathway 6: Classic Growth via Product/Service Improvement, I've assumed that in year 3 we have a new product being launched. So that results in big gains of new accounts in years 3 and 4 tailing off in year 5. It does a similar thing in Growth Pathway 8: Classic New Account Addition, but since we are always acquiring new accounts it's not as dramatic. Pathway 14: Existing Customer Product Migration is a dramatic growth plan, but shows the inverse of adoption rates to Pathway 6, since it will take time to migrate accounts to the new offering. This has two impacts when you look at the financials. First, let's look at how it shows up in annual revenues for the company (Figure 12.4).

Revenue Model

> Input expected revenue breakout by year, by pathway. This will translate into charts and should total 100%. Cells with blue text…

Growth Pathways	Percentage of Revenues per Pathway	Pathway Revenue Breakout	5 Year Plan Year 1	Year 2	Year 3	Year 4	Year 5	Total
1. Pure innovation testbed	0%	$ -	20% / $ -	20% / $ -	20% / $ -	20% / $ -	20% / $ -	100%
2. Offensive market disruption	0%	$ -	20% / $ -	20% / $ -	20% / $ -	20% / $ -	20% / $ -	100%
3. Testbed for disruption	0%	$ -	20% / $ -	20% / $ -	20% / $ -	20% / $ -	20% / $ -	100%
4. Geographic expansion	0%	$ -	20% / $ -	20% / $ -	20% / $ -	20% / $ -	20% / $ -	100%
5. Innovation share grab	0%	$ -	20% / $ -	20% / $ -	20% / $ -	20% / $ -	20% / $ -	100%
6. Classic growth via product/ service improvement	4%	$ 80,000,000	0% / $ -	0% / $ -	50% / $ 40,000,000	40% / $ 32,000,000	10% / $ 8,000,000	100%
7. Introduction of disruptive business model	0%	$ -	20% / $ -	20% / $ -	20% / $ -	20% / $ -	20% / $ -	100%
8. Classic new account addition	16%	$ 320,000,000	10% / $ 32,000,000	10% / $ 32,000,000	35% / $ 112,000,000	25% / $ 80,000,000	20% / $ 64,000,000	100%
9. Disruptive innovation	0%	$ -	20% / $ -	20% / $ -	20% / $ -	20% / $ -	20% / $ -	100%
10. Regionally focused new product development	0%	$ -	20% / $ -	20% / $ -	20% / $ -	20% / $ -	20% / $ -	100%
11. Align with regional contracting practices	0%	$ -	20% / $ -	20% / $ -	20% / $ -	20% / $ -	20% / $ -	100%
12. Classic geographic expansion	0%	$ -	20% / $ -	20% / $ -	20% / $ -	20% / $ -	20% / $ -	100%
13. Transformational innovation	0%	$ -	20% / $ -	20% / $ -	20% / $ -	20% / $ -	20% / $ -	100%
14. Existing customer product migration	16%	$ 320,000,000	0% / $ -	0% / $ -	20% / $ 64,000,000	30% / $ 96,000,000	50% / $ 160,000,000	100%
15. Offer new acquisition models	0%	$ -	20% / $ -	20% / $ -	20% / $ -	20% / $ -	20% / $ -	100%
16. "Milking the cow"	64%	$ 1,280,000,000	20% / $ 256,000,000	20% / $ 256,000,000	20% / $ 256,000,000	20% / $ 256,000,000	20% / $ 256,000,000	100%
Total		$ 2,000,000,000	$ 288,000,000	$ 288,000,000	$ 472,000,000	$ 464,000,000	$ 488,000,000	

FIGURE 12.3 Revenue Model

Total Revenues per Plan Year

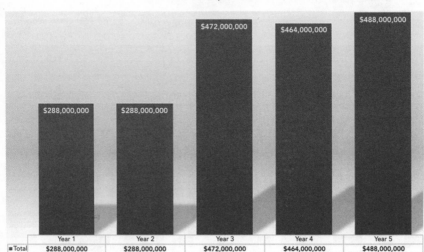

■Total	Year 1	Year 2	Year 3	Year 4	Year 5
	$288,000,000	$288,000,000	$472,000,000	$464,000,000	$488,000,000

FIGURE 12.4   Total Revenues per Plan Year

Our assumptions show a significant improvement due to the planned launch starting in year 3. By pathway we can also see how the revenues are allocated by year (Figure 12.5).

When we get to the financial modeling part of our process, we will use these breakouts by year and by pathway to drive investment/expected ROI.

Is There a Way to Assign Different "New" versus "Existing" Weightings by Branch in the Decision Tree?

I often hear, "Using the top-down Four Key Questions approach is fast, but it forces me to use the same breakouts on independent branches." Another good question. The answer is, of course, yes, you can assign weightings. You simply need the branch weighting by node to sum to 100 in your model.

If you did this process part right – had clear goals, had good representation from across functional leadership, allowed a structured and open discourse, came to a generally accepted outcome across participants – then you truly have something powerful: a clear approach that harnesses the collective wisdom and experience of the leadership team that will be executing on it. This is the foundation of success.

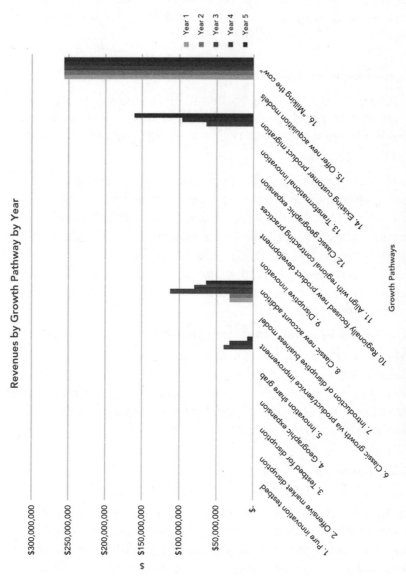

FIGURE 12.5   Revenues by Growth Pathway by Year

Principles of Use

The principles when using the tool are the same for all businesses, whether a large company or small. And they follow some simple themes:

1. **Focus on the critical stuff.**

   Maslow had it right with his hierarchy. You need to focus on the most critical parts of what you could do to survive. Using the Growth Framework, those critical areas quickly become clear.

2. **Kill the bad bets.**

   Look, you could do anything you choose to do as a growth strategist. Learning to ignore the bad bets is incredibly important. Don't fall in love with the romance of disruption if it isn't necessary. Disruption is, well, disruptive! And messy. And fraught with risk. If you are unlikely to have success, then stay away from it. Also, why waste time on pathways you cannot execute on? If you don't have the resources to develop a new product, then focus on what you do have the resources to do.

3. **Use the "gray areas" to drive evolution.**

   When you do exercises like this, the winners and losers are very clear. The hard part is sifting through the murky or gray areas. A critical factor in considering these areas is to think about forcing evolution into the model. By evolution, I mean cellular change. Fundamental shift in the practices of the business to drive longer-term success.

4. **Do some math.**

   Math is the universal language and done right has teeth! Finishing off with agreed-to revenue breakouts by pathway is critical to generate confidence in our plans to achieve goal. Knowing what we are trying to accomplish by pathway from a revenue standpoint is necessary for the next part of our process.

13

Select Strategies

Step 5: Plan the Battle on Each Route

The selection of a subset of the 16 Growth Pathways that we generated in Step 4 now will drive the creation of the actual strategies and tactics to be employed by the team.

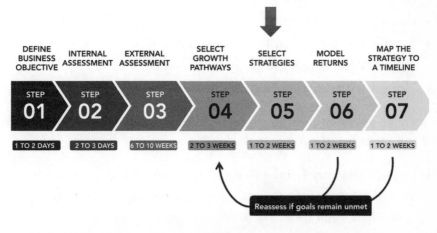

There are many books written about strategy, and what it is and isn't. Strategy answers the question "how" we will achieve our goals. Tactics are the "means" we will use, the measurable "who does what, where, and when" that makes the strategy real. So growth strategies (which are what this book is about) are clean statements about how the company will grow, and growth tactics are specific actions to achieve growth.

James Klein of Qorvo has a great perspective on growth strategy:

> Strategy is not what you are doing for the rest of the year. A strategy is what you want to be. What do you want to do in 3 to 5 years? Often, one of the first things I like to do, and you know this because we did it with you, is to try to establish a goal and it ought to be a **scary** goal. When we formed the company, we said we want to double the business in 4 years, and if you do that math you go, that's crazy, right? And we failed...It took us 5 years.
>
> Having that aggressive goal out there to try to understand where you want to go, I think it's really important, so you know to the new practitioner, figure out what you want to be, put a goal out there, and have a strategy to get there.

Some growth strategy examples you might see from the Fortune 200:

- Enter new adjacent markets.
- Take share from incumbents.
- Introduce a new consumption-based business model.
- Leverage brand to drive adoption.
- Use existing customers to create a new market.
- Bundle new product with existing commodity.
- Hotel California: easy adoption with high exit costs.
- Monetize existing intellectual property.

Those are all growth strategies. *Growth tactics* reside below them. For the same list, they may look like this:

- Growth Strategy 1: Take share from incumbents.
  - Growth Tactic 1: Create a marketing campaign highlighting product differences/our unique value.

- Growth Tactic 2: Target financial incentives for new customers.
- Growth Tactic 3: Create new acquisition models, moving from CapEx to OpEx.
- Growth Strategy 2: Enter new adjacent markets.
  - Growth Tactic 1: Acquire existing branded provider in market.
  - Growth Tactic 2: Expand sales team training and portfolio to address adjacent market.
  - Growth Tactic 3: Refocus marketing dollars to support adjacent market entry.
- Growth Strategy 3: Introduce a new consumption-based business model.
  - Growth Tactic 1: Study best-in-class consumption-based practices.
  - Growth Tactic 2: Build background infrastructure to monitor/ manage usage.
  - Growth Tactic 3: Create a compensation system to support refocusing of sales staff. ·
- Growth Strategy 4: Leverage brand to drive adoption.
  - Growth Tactic 1: Create campaign messaging aligning brand equity of past products with new offering.
  - Growth Tactic 2: Target marquee customers for visible deployment.
  - Growth Tactic 3: Use existing customers to create a new market.

When you think about planning a growth strategy, you have to collide all of the factors we've put into our process so far: the goal, the team, its capabilities, resourcing, the market landscape, and competitive forces. What are the different ways could we achieve our aim?

Let's talk about the practical process to generate these strategies and tactics.

I'm writing this section for practitioners who are leading a team effort, but you can do these steps as an individual practitioner as well.

Our goal in this step is to harness the diversity of thought, experience, and independent intellectual horsepower of our team. We also want to achieve the dual process of team cohesion and collaboration.

Form the team into groups of no more than three members each. Try to make the teams people who don't always work together or combine the most visible cheerleaders with the most visible naysayers. The goal is diversity of thought and acknowledgment of challenge.

Give each team a copy of work done to date. Goal definition needs to be formally reviewed. This drives EVERYTHING. Provide the synopsis of each of the prior phases: internal assessment, external assessment, selected pathways, and their associated financial aims by year. These are all the ingredients we need to make a great strategy.

Then give each team a stack of blank paper and some pencils. This is meant to be an old-school, tactile exercise. If you have to do this remotely, use online collaboration tools. Ask them to each individually develop strategies to achieve the revenue aims **by pathway.** High-level bullets. Action focused. Three to five high-level strategies per pathway. This step should take no more than an hour. Don't let them get too detailed and keep them focused on the goal.

Within each group, have them review their strategies with their teammates individually.

Facilitate a Q&A by person. Why do they believe their strategies will achieve their goal? Are there obvious strategies that you would have expected to see? Offer them to the team and get their reactions . . . there may be a reason they are omitting them. Facilitate their thought process but leverage the knowledge and expertise of the teams. Make non-Marketers consider a Marketing strategy. Have Marketers consider Product Development and R&D strategy. The goal is diversity of thought and mutual appreciation of the challenges by role of achieving the goals.

Strategy Development Classics to Consider

Here are a few big strategy decisions the team will have to think through by pathway.

Pricing Strategy

You know the old saying . . . you can have it two of three ways: good, fast, or cheap. You choose the two. Who are you in the market? What will your strategy lend itself to? Premium brand, premium price, premium quality? Value brand, low price, low quality? Knowing who you are, and who the market will let you be is important as you consider the team's strategy and tactics.

Build or Buy: Organic versus Inorganic Growth

This is one of the most important decisions. Build (organic) or buy (acquire) is both a financial and operational decision. Do you have the ability to acquire? Do you have access to capital? If not, then unless you are willing to take on significant debt or do a reverse acquisition (where the seller finances the sale), or merge firms, then this is off the table. For most large companies, this is a typical part of their playbook. They need acquisitions to drive near-term revenues and to accelerate the breadth of their portfolios. Nancy Lyons Callahan talked about this approach at SAP:

> The classic scenario that's played out at SAP, which is quite public, is that to accelerate the range of cloud offerings that we have, SAP has had a very successful acquisition strategy for the last 8 to 10 years . . . to bring these new offerings in-house and then to very successfully sell those new offerings to existing customers.

Remember, Nancy is in the services world, and prior to the pandemic, the US unemployment rate was below 5%, and we have an aging population. Organic growth in services is really difficult if you are a company of scale.

In the Professional Services world, there are basically three kinds of inorganic approach you will see play out: financial acquirer, merger of firms, strategic acquisition. A financial acquirer is basically an investor purchase of a services firm. Whether it's private equity or a roll-up of a larger firm looking to increase its revenue line, their intent is focused on ROI and the ability of the entity to both produce revenue in the near term and for PE firms to grow and sell at a later date. Mergers happen when firms are looking for stability or want to grow without coming up with funds for a major acquisition. Strategics are acquirers who value IP, geographic footprint, and long-run potential contributions. Sometimes it's a tech firm that wants more access to the C-Suite (think EDS acquisition of A.T. Kearney). Other times it's an international firm looking to open an office in a new geography. The expectation is that it is cheaper and easier to acquire an ongoing business than to organically grow one.

As you move into maker economies, found in the hardware, software, OEM/ODM world, the choice becomes harder because manufacturing requires standardization of process for quality/efficiency. Building is often the best approach at that point, unless you are hoping to acquire the product portfolio an existing company already produces.

Product Strategy: Sizzle versus Steak

In every industry there are companies that are marketing led versus engineering led. Some companies sell on "sizzle," or the promise of what's to come. Others on "steak," or the capability of what they make. Product strategy needs to consider when to pull the trigger on innovation. If you wait to announce until you have perfection, you leave the door open for a competitor to preempt you in the market. Announce too early, and you risk disappointing the market with underwhelming product performance.

Lead versus Follow

Everyone wants to be a market leader, right? Well, just because you don't lead in the creation of a market doesn't mean you can't dominate it. Early movers, market leaders have a very heavy lift. Feels a lot like new customer acquisition. Super-weighty, long payback cycle, high risk. But you are the market creator, so you get to call lots of shots. Late entrants, however, have to be really disruptive to take share. You need to have a better mousetrap. I talked a bit about this with Sue Spradley, CEO of Motion Intelligence. By any standard, Sue is one of the most accomplished business professionals you will ever be lucky enough to meet. In addition to her CEO role, Sue is also on the Board of Directors at Avaya and Qorvo corporations. A Telecom industry executive, Sue was CEO and Chairman of the Board at US ignite, a White House and National Science Foundation initiative focused on the applications for smart-city implementation. Prior to US ignite, Sue was president of the North American region at Nokia Siemens Networks, where she served as an Executive Board Member. Earlier, she served in a variety of roles at Nortel, most recently as President of its Global Services division. Sue is smart, insightful, and forthright with her position on things. I was really excited to have her participate in the book. Back to "late entrants" and Sue's take on one of her early roles as a growth strategist:

> Nortel entered extremely late into this market, and to say that the market was saturated was an understatement. It was an interesting market because it was saturated, but people didn't like the product! So even though there are big names with big solutions, people weren't that thrilled with the product they had. My job was to come in and figure out how to introduce our product to enter that market. I was blessed because I worked for a guy who was just a kind of crazy genius. He really knew his stuff, and he came out of the finance world. He kept saying, "I think you've got to change the game," and that's what we did.

Channel Strategy: Direct versus Indirect

How will you sell to your customers? I know this seems like an obvious answer, but just because you've always reached your customers one way doesn't mean that you should always do that. If you are an entrepreneur at my favorite coffee shop, "Joe's," you might think that selling direct to customers is all you can do. Not true. Example: Find a company that does gift baskets and offer those homemade donuts as part of their offering. Or list your products on Uber Eats to get your coffee and food sold through and delivered by an Uber driver.

For corporate clients that sell through channel partners, this is a really tough challenge that I've advised on over the past 30 years. At what point do you go direct? There is tremendous fear involved here. All money comes from customers, but not all companies touch those customers directly. If you've always sold through a channel, will you upset your partners by going direct? Will they move to sell a competitor's brand? Can you handle the challenges of fulfillment to individual customers if you aren't built to do that? Can you stand up a sales force to serve that customer community? John Seebeck talked previously about how dramatic the impact of direct to customer through a digital channel was for Crate & Barrel. Are you ready for that journey?

Product Portfolio: Focus versus Expansion

Has your company been in business for a long time? If so, you probably have a big product portfolio to pull from. Many times that can lead to a lack of focus as SKUs stack up over time. Focus can become a critical part of your strategy at that point. Newer companies, or those pursuing new market areas, need to consider expansion and how best to access growth opportunities.

Leverage Existing or Hire

When you consider how you will grow, you have to consider whether you will use existing or hire new personnel to handle the workload. Specifically, I mean you have to decide whether or not to retask people who are focused on current activities that were the strategy you established in the past few years. If you are going to retask them, what impact will that have on planned revenues? If you need to hire new, what will that cost?

Train Existing or Hire

A close corollary to the last question is considering whether the current workforce is capable of the new tasks you will set in front of them. I wasn't in the room when Microsoft decided to deploy 365, but you can bet there was an execution challenge when trying to teach people who sold product through a channel to sell a service directly. Every company that considers a move to solution versus product sales faces this, and the reality is that not every team member will be able to make that shift.

Once the team has come up with their strategies individually, consolidate them. Identify the "no brainer," or generally accepted strategies, and then focus conversation on the ones that are unique. Keep some, kill some, but end up with a list of things that the team collectively buys into.

Take a breath; this is a major milestone that the team has reached.

Now have each team pitch their strategy deck to the group. Open the floor to Q&A. Get a good critical discussion going. What will work, what won't, why? Get each functional lead to try to shoot down the plan from their perspective. What are their concerns? What existing priorities need to shift?

This drill is a bit of a balancing act. You need to unearth all potential barriers to strategies that could become a block to success. Have the Vetoers be vocal. Make sure the Doers buy into their respective tasks. Get to the challenges that you have to think through as a group.

At the same time, you don't want to dishearten the group by only pointing out flaws. There is guaranteed to be brilliance and creative thought in this exercise. So while we celebrate the agreement across teams, we need to discuss the challenges.

At this point, you as leader should take all the strategy decks and consolidate them into a single plan. See what aligns and what doesn't.

If you are doing this process by yourself as an entrepreneur, this is a good time to share your thinking with two kinds of people: those who know and those who don't.

Those who know are colleagues and will understand the nuance of what you are writing down and the business behind it. Those who don't are friends or family members who don't work with you, but whom you trust. Both groups can help you highlight areas to improve your plan. Colleagues will know practical/detailed challenges to your plan. Friends and family will force you to simplify your world until it makes sense to them – on that journey you will identify holes/gaps/logical fails in your plan. Both are extremely useful.

If you are doing this as part of the larger team, you present a consolidated final set of strategies that represents the curation of individual thought from every team member based on our goals, capabilities, customer assessment, competitor threat, and regulatory and economic reality.

Once you have sign-off from the group, you are ready for the heavy lift of tactics.

Good tactics translate general strategies to action statements done by people at a certain time, with a certain, measurable cost. By creating measurable, assignable tactics we create a plan that is actionable and has a quantifiable cost. That will be really important in Chapter 14 where we calculate financials.

Have the teams break out again and work to define tactics to support each initiative.

Grind through objections to resource constraints (people, money, time, equipment use). Each functional area will have concerns as high-level strategies become practical tasks. Budgets will be shifted, headcounts reassigned, business unit charters shifted. Legal, HR, and any other function that objects to how things will be done should throw a flag at this point. Facilitate a discussion to get to a reasonable outcome.

No one said it would be easy, but when you have done this step you will have created your battle plan.

14

Model Returns

Step 6: Assess the Outcome

Here's where our process differentiates from most planning processes. We are going to put teeth into our plan.

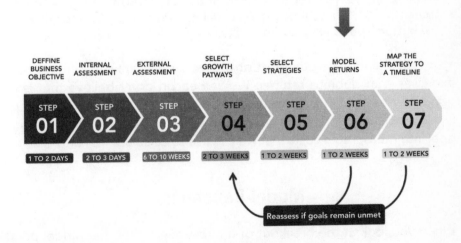

Most growth strategy is pie in the sky. Some creatives think about market-facing activity without an appreciation for what that exercise will cost. I personally reject that approach. Growth *has* to be profitable, sustainable, and scalable for any-sized company for it to be worth pursuing.

John Seebeck, James Klein, and Rob Hays add their own beliefs on the role of profitability.

John Seebeck, VP and GM of e-Commerce at CDW:

> When you run a store, or a group of stores, your job is very simple. It's to grow profitably. It's the same in retail. At Crate & Barrel it's very, very simple . . . the targets are always profitable net revenues.

James Klein, President Infrastructure and Defense at Qorvo:

> We certainly want to grow, but we want to have some boundary conditions. Growth without profit is not very exciting. . . So yes, you want to have growth, but you want to make sure that you're also able to grow the bottom line. And my model has always been to try to grow expenses at half the rate we're growing revenue – then we can glide into a continuous improvement bottom-line profitability. When it's all said and done, that's the game, right? It's all about how much profit you can put toward the bottom line.

Rob Hays, VP and Chief Strategy Officer at Lenovo:

> It's all about the finances at the end of the day. People argue that it's strategic . . . Okay, so if its strategic, tell me how that's going to fall to the bottom line? You've got to always bring it back to that.

Understand this truth: Most growth strategies are soft, amorphous exercises with dubious returns. We at Beacon don't believe that is a good way to get the organization to execute on our plan. Every step in our process has led to this point: converting the action to achieve our goal into measurable costs that we can use to calculate ROI or profit.

Model Revenues

When you look at the breakout of the revenue target, the model puts a single number at the end of each pathway. However, we know that this model needs to have a more detailed breakout by planning period. Since most growth strategies have a 5-year time horizon, let's use that as a rule.

This phase in our larger process depends largely on the finance function. From a change management standpoint, it's critical that this analysis has the support and credibility that finance can provide. By engaging them throughout this step we get a high degree of confidence in the math and the output of our model. We also need the model to fit the culture/standards of the company we are working with or are a part of.

So, our first process step is to convert the revenue goal by pathway into an annual goal. The easiest way to do this is to assign percentages of growth that you plan on *by year*. Note – this isn't a static/standard breakout. There is an incredible amount of flux based on the pathway, the maturity of the product/services, the competitive landscape, and the resourcing that will be put behind the initiative. That said, the team should come to an agreement on what is reasonable for planning purposes.

Joe's Coffee

I've created a hypothetical case to illustrate this process step. These are EXACTLY the same steps you would take within your larger company as you execute, and this approach is based on the 1,500+ projects we've delivered as a firm.

It's December 31st – New Year's Eve – and Cameron was planning for her future. She has always dreamed of opening a coffee shop, has saved her money, and now needs to build out a plan to make it a reality. By nature, she's pretty conservative with her needs and is thinking through her 5-year growth plan. So far, she's gone through our process and has come up with the following breakout over the 5-year time frame:

- 70% of her revenues will come from existing customers. She knows she still has to work hard to get new customers that will become existing customers over that time frame.
- 100% will come from her single location, since she's going to have her hands full just opening and running that one spot.

- 80% will come from existing goods and services, because she wants to offer music and book readings at some point.

- 100% will come through existing business models. At this point she doesn't want to get fancy with loyalty points or subscription-based coffee, although she may revisit that next year as she looks at how she did against plan.

- Her aggregate 5-year goal is $1,500,000 in revenues, with an overall profit of at least $65k/year for her living expenses, although she can self-fund for 1 year.

Cameron sat down and populated the framework per our process and generated what her 5-year model looked like. Her framework output showed a clear focus on a couple of key pathways (Figure 14.1).

Out of 16 potential ways to grow the top line, she's killed 12. This is really good news for a sole practitioner just starting out. So she has to worry about only four things: milking the cow, new account addition, getting existing customers to try new things, and attracting people to her shop with cool new stuff.

Here's another way to look at the model output, that clearly shows the four areas of focus for Cameron to achieve her plan (Figure 14.2).

This aligns well with her initial thinking about the importance of satisfying existing customers and adding new ones (Pathways 16 and 8). It also means that she's going to generate more revenue by selling an existing customer something new than she is by trying to attract new customers with a new offering. It's an interesting insight that is borne out across our clients.

The next step in our modeling process is to distribute the revenues by pathway over the 5-year period so we can both plan our income and also align investment.

To do that, she has to assign a "revenue curve" to the gross number. That is, for years 1– 5, what percentage of total revenue in that pathway is earned that year?

Growth Framework Output

Created for **Joe's Coffee**

Color coding represents relative attractiveness of each pathway.

The darker the revenue percentage and target revenues are, the better it is for you. Medium gray pathways require discussion. Optimal pathways are bolded.

Customer	Geography	Offering	Business Model	Percentage of Revenues per Pathway	Target Revenues per Pathway	Growth Pathways
		20% New Offering	0% New Model	0%	$ -	1. Pure innoation testbed
	0% New Geo		100% Existing Model	0%	$ -	2. Offensive market disruption
		80% Existing Offering	0% New Model	0%	$ -	3. Testbed for disruption
30% New Customer			100% Existing Model	0%	$ -	4. Geographic expansion
		20% New Offering	0% New Model	0%	$ -	5. Innovation share grab
	100% Existing Geo		100% Existing Model	6.00%	$ 90,000	6. Classic growth ia product/service improvement
		80% Existing Offering	0% New Model	0%	$ -	7. Introduction of disruptive business model
			100% Existing Model	24.00%	$ 360,000	8. Classic new account addition

NEW GROWTH

$1,500,000 Growth Goal

		20% New Offering	0% New Model	0%	$ -	9. Disruptive innovation
	0% New Geo		100% Existing Model	0%	$ -	10. Regionally focused new product development
		80% Existing Offering	0% New Model	0%	$ -	11. Align with regional contracting practices
70% Existing Customer			100% Existing Model	0%	$ -	12. Classic geographic expansion
		20% New Offering	0% New Model	0%	$ -	13. Transformational innovation
	100% Existing Geo		100% Existing Model	14.00%	$ 210,000	14. Existing customer product migration
		80% Existing Offering	0% New Model	0%	$ -	15. Offer new acquisition models
			100% Existing Model	56.00%	$ 840,000	16. "Milking the cow"

DEFEND AND GROW

Total	100%	$ 1,500,000,00

FIGURE 14.1 Growth Framework Output

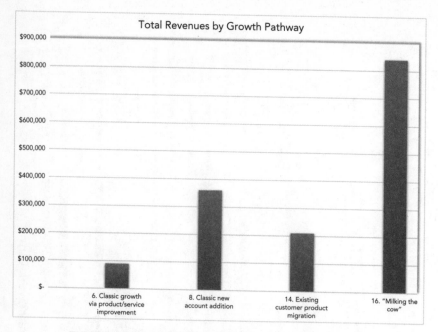

FIGURE 14.2   Total Revenues by Growth Pathway

I like the model Cameron has built. She made a few assumptions.

1. Year 1 would be a slow open, focused on getting new customers and establishing them as existing customers (Pathways 8 and 16).

2. Year 2, she would attract the same number of new customers (Pathway 8) and keep the majority as existing customers (Pathway 16).

3. Year 3 the business will be stable enough for her to offer new things to her customers, which are reflected in new customers (Pathway 6) and selling more to existing customers (Pathway 14).

4. At no time in this 5-year window is she contemplating geographic expansion.

In fact, she isn't planning on anything new and innovative until year 3. She's mapped out her annual assumptions, as shown in Figure 14.3.

Revenue Model

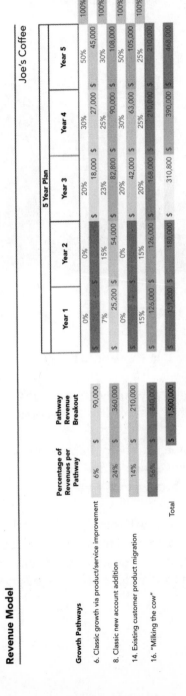

FIGURE 14.3   Revenue Model

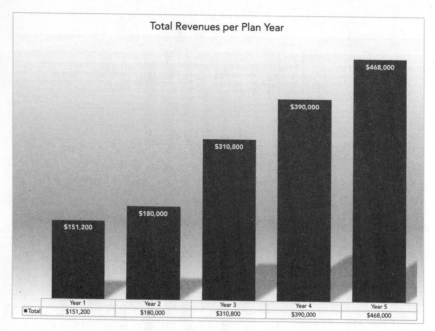

FIGURE 14.4   Total Revenues per Plan Year

Figure 14.4 shows this more intuitively as you look at revenues by year.

So the company will start slowly on revenues at $150k/year, scaling to $468k by year 5, which seems like a reasonable distribution of the revenues.

Her application of a curve to her pathway gross numbers not only gives the annual revenues of the business in aggregate but also gives the revenues by pathway by year. Figure 14.5 shows what that looks like.

If you look closely you will see that only Pathways 8 and 16 have revenues associated with year 1. Her job will be getting new customers and turning them into repeat customers. Pathways 6 and 14 kick in year 3, which allows us to plan for new services and offerings after the start-up phase.

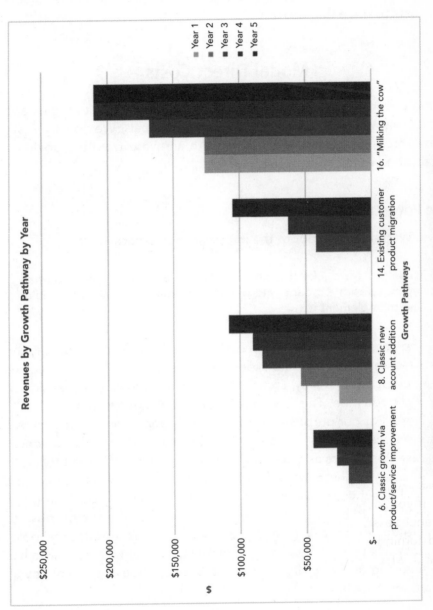

FIGURE 14.5 Revenues by Growth Pathway by Year

Cameron has done a nice job getting the top line established.

Now it's time to move onto the part of our process that considers the costs to drive that growth.

Model Direct Costs

In the previous chapter, as a team, you built out your strategies and tactics that will be employed to achieve your goals. We now translate that exercise to our financial model with an eye toward the goals we established at the start of our journey.

The Power of Tactics

Kevin Watters talked about the importance of tactics in planning:

> I used to make a joke that you had to be "Stratical," right? You had to come up with a great strategy and understand tactically how you're going to implement it

The unsung hero of this process – tactics – allows us to quantify the cost. Tactics allows us to consider the trade-offs of direct cost versus benefit. Put another way, tactics trigger an analysis of the cost side of the profit equation. This lets us calculate the ROI of strategy.

Note: For our purposes, we care mostly about direct costs. Direct costs are costs that can be attributed directly to a particular action, in this case, the tactics associated with our strategies. We aren't trying to model every expense in the business or its pre existing overhead, just material direct controllable costs associated with our growth strategy. While we could build all costs in, it's not necessary for the purpose of the strategy exercise. We need order of magnitude, not decimal point accuracy. That said, if you have a great finance team member who has the time and desire to dig deeply into the cost side of the plan, by all means let them have at it . . .

This is a process step where finance is engaged to help build out the appropriate cost model for your business. In our example, we are simplifying for Joe's Coffee, but I've had clients build extremely robust models over the years.

Let's think about the drivers of direct, quantifiable cost: people (full-time equivalents, or FTEs), nonrecurring expense (NRE), advertising spend, marketing spend, manufacturing/operations. These are the major cost buckets we need to consider.

People

One of the largest cost buckets for most businesses is HR. When you assign a task, you assign it to a person. That person is either trained or untrained for the task. If trained, chances are they are busy with their time doing something else. If untrained, they need to be educated about their new role. So how do you put a price on their engagement? Well – start with how many bodies you think it will take. These are FTEs (full time equivalents). Your finance team should be working with you on this, and they can help you proxy the cost of FTEs as you think about supporting the execution of a tactic. Then add in the training component, or the opportunity cost of a repositioning.

The tricky part of this is that people are not a product. You can't assume that you can immediately replace or hire someone in a job. So, there is a time component to this. Whether you are hiring someone new or you are asking an existing employee to do something new, there is a lag as they are either onboarded or transition from the current work they are doing. But make no mistake about it: Tasks require people, and people cost money!

NRE (Nonrecurring Expense)

This is a bucket that happens only once. Typically with product development, this is a one-time expense that you incur as you develop a product, such as R&D or an engineering expense or something to do with the development of a marketing campaign. As you think about the creative aspect of new product introduction, NRE is a focal point you need to consider. Sometimes this overlaps with the FTE calculation.

Advertising Spend

This spend is a very specific line item. It's the spend that happens as you execute a marketing plan. This is the dollars you spend for clicks, minutes of ad time, billboards, sponsorship, etc. Advertising is very important in several of the classic parts of market shaping.

Awareness. Advertising lets people know you exist!

Desire. Good advertising makes people want to acquire your goods or services.

Differentiation. Advertising is a great way to show why/how you are different than the norm.

What's great about advertising today is that unlike prior generations that were only broadcast in nature, today you can have interactive or measured digital experiences. Google AdWords or Google Trends are really amazing tools that didn't exist a decade ago. Facebook and Instagram are simple pathways to customers of interest. It doesn't matter the size of company, targeted personalized advertising is available to all and very easy to quantify.

Marketing Spend

Marketing encompasses the activities associated with creating demand in the market. Advertising, messaging, target product profiling, competitive positioning, demand creation, hype/buzz...These are all critical elements of growth.

Manufacturing/Operations

Once you have demand and a designed product, you have to build and inventory it. The manufacturing cost of a new opportunity needs to be considered. There are plenty of financial metrics about this that should be thought about, but at a high level you need to assess the total cost of operations to enable the new strategy that was identified.

Cameron came up with the following strategies and tactics when she worked through our process:

Pathway 6: Classic Growth via Product/Service Improvement

Strategy 1: Expand offerings for Evenings and Arts series.

Tactic 1: Extend hours Friday and Saturday night till 11 pm.

Tactic 2: Friday night Jazz series

Tactic 3: Saturday night open-mike poetry

Tactic 4: Advertise locally and digitally.

Strategy 2: Offer Sunday farmers market.

Tactic 1: Rent parking lot space to vendors.

Tactic 2: Advertise on local media and digitally.

Tactic 3: Flyer handouts to customers

Pathway 8: Classic New Account Addition

Strategy 1: Create digital marketing campaign.

Tactic 1: Weekly post on happenings in store

Tactic 2: User photo promotions

Tactic 3: Daily music playlist and likes

Tactic 4: Connect with other local businesses.

Strategy 2: Add sidewalk signage.

Tactic 1: Decorate street-facing façade to be inviting for passersby.

Tactic 2: Daily chalkboard

Tactic 3: Flyer handouts

Pathway 14: Existing Customer Product Migration

Strategy 1: Communicate new expanded offerings for Evenings and Arts series.

Tactic 1: Communicate news with every customer at point of trans-action.

Tactic 2: Notice of new offerings on printed receipts

Tactic 3: In-store signage

Tactic 4: Digital communication through social media and email

Pathway 16: Milking the Cow

Strategy 1: Maintain high-quality physical store environment.

Tactic 1: Daily evaluation of furnishings for wear/damage

Tactic 2: Hourly cleaning

Tactic 3: Daily window cleaning

Tactic 4: Idea box for customers to identify issues with facility

Strategy 2: Maintain high-quality product.

Tactic 1: Rigorous training for new hires on customer service and product prep

Tactic 2: Provide freshness guarantee.

Tactic 3: No-questions-asked redo policy

Strategy 3: Implement loyalty program.

Tactic 1: Stamped card program for free coffee

Tactic 2: Priority line for loyalty program customers

Tactic 3: Digital communication with enrolled customers

Lots of good stuff here that we should unpack from a process standpoint. Let's see how this works by digging into the first pathway: Pathway 6. Cameron had created strategies and tactics in the earlier phase.

Now the drill is to assign costs to each tactic. So, Cameron would populate the tactics like this:

Pathway 6: Classic Growth via Product/Service Improvement

Strategy 1: Expand offerings for Evenings and Arts series.

Tactic 1: Extend hours Friday and Saturday night till 11 pm

Hourly wages for 2 employees @$17/hour, 8 hours per day,
2 nights per week, 52 weeks per year = $28,288

Tactic 2: Friday night Jazz series

Stage, speaker, and lighting build-out = $15,000
Band Fees = $800/week, 52 weeks = $41,600

Tactic 3: Saturday night open-mike poetry

No additional cost – included above

Tactic 4: Advertise locally and digitally.

$50/week – Facebook/Insta adverts, 52 weeks = $2,600
$10/week flyer printout, 52 weeks = $520

Strategy 2: Sunday farmers market

Total expected costs (summing following tactic breakout) = $3,536

Tactic 1: Rent parking lot space to vendors.

1 hourly employee, $17/hour, 4 hours, 52 weeks = $3,536

Tactic 2: Advertise on local media and digitally.

No additional cost, included above

Tactic 3: Flyer handouts to customers

No additional cost, included above

So, we have a good sense of the cost of our growth tactics. This allows us to do something very rare in the world of growth strategy: We can calculate ROI.

Practically, your finance team should take point on this, but you can do a rough calculation yourself (if you don't have a finance team!).

Use the profit equation:

Profit = Revenue – Cost

In our process we know that revenues are given as an overarching goal and then are broken out by pathway. Cost is measured by investments at the growth tactic line:

Profit (ROI) = Revenues (Pathway) – Cost (Strategy/Tactics/Pathway)

So we can measure both gross profit (total Revenues – total Costs) and profit by pathway, which is really powerful.

Let's keep using Pathway 6. We know from our original work that our estimate of revenue for all 5 years is $90,000.

We also know that if you add up expenses per year, you have $91,536 in year 1, decreasing to $76,536 year 2 (because stage/speakers/lights are NREs). Since we only work to expand services starting in year 3 and there is a slower ramp-up to capacity, the revenues and costs line up as shown in Table 14.1.

This analysis shows that while our strategies may be creative and logically good, they are too expensive to achieve the goal. She's losing a ton of money each year! Yikes!

Table 14.1   Growth Pathway ROI Model

		Growth Pathway ROI Model			
Revenues	Y1	Y2	Y3	Y4	Y5
Pathway 6: New Customer Acquisition Revenues	0	0	18,000	27,000	45,000
Total Revenue	0	0	18,000	27,000	45,000
Expenses					
Strategy 1: Evening Arts					
Tactic 1 - Extended hours			28,288	28,288	28,288
Tactic 2 - Friday night Jazz					
Band fees			41,600	41,600	41,600
Stage build			15,000		
Tactic 3: Open mike					
Tactic 4 - Advertise locally and digitally					
Facebook/Instagram			2,600	2,600	2,600
Flyer printout			520	520	520
Strategy 2: Sunday Farmers Market					
Tactic 1: Rent space to vendors			3,536	3,536	3,536
Tactic 2: Advertise locally and digitally					
Tactic 3: Flyer handout					
Total Expense	0	0	88,008	73,008	73,008
ROI	0	0	(70,008)	(46,008)	(28,008)

Table 14.2 Growth Pathway ROI Model Results

Revenues	Growth Pathway ROI Model				
	Y1	Y2	Y3	Y4	Y5
Pathway 6: New Customer Acquisition Revenues	0	0	18,000	27,000	45,000
Total Revenue	0	0	18,000	27,000	45,000
Expenses Strategy 1: Evening Arts					
Tactic 1 - Extended hours			28,288	28,288	28,288
Tactic 2 - Friday night Jazz					
Stage build			15,000		
Tactic 3: Open mike					
Tactic 4 - Advertise locally and digitally					
Facebook/Instagram			2,600	2,600	2,600
Flyer printout			520	520	520
Strategy 2: Sunday Farmers Market					
Tactic 1: Rent space to vendors			3,536	3,536	3,536
Tactic 2: Advertise locally and digitally					
Tactic 3: Flyer handout					
Total Expense	0	3	46,408	31,408	31,408
ROI	0	0	(28,408)	(4,408)	13,592

A review of assumptions shows the culprit can be found in band costs for Friday night Jazz. It's just too expensive to have that offering. Cameron's a pretty smart person, so she decides instead to make it an open-mike night for local musicians. This will be just like the book and poetry readings the following night – only this will be for musicians. That will draw in locals and hopefully people will self-select out if they aren't any good!

That knocks off $41,600 per year from our math. Let's see the result, which is shown in Table 14.2.

It's a little better, but it's still a loser. Walk away?

Cameron looks at her model again and realizes that she forgot to consider that all new things she is offering to acquire new customers in Pathway 6 are the EXACT things that will be used to access the revenues in Pathway 14, selling to existing customers!

Table 14.3 Growth Pathway ROI Model (Pathway 14)

			Growth Pathway ROI Model		
Revenues		Y1	Y2	Y3	Y4	Y5
	Pathway 6: New Customer Acquisition Revenues	0	0	18,000	27,000	45,000
	Pathway 14: Existing Customer Product Migration Revenues	0	0	42,000	63,000	105,000
	Total Revenue	**0**	**0**	**60,000**	**90,000**	**150,000**
Expenses						
	Strategy 1: Evening Arts					
	Tactic 1 - Extended hours			28,288	28,288	28,288
	Tactic 2 - Friday night Jazz					
	Stage build			15,000		
	Tactic 3: Open mike					
	Tactic 4 - Advertise locally and digitally					
	Facebook/Instagram			2,600	2,600	2,600
	Flyer printout			520	520	520
	Strategy 2: Sunday Farmers Market					
	Tactic 1: Rent space to vendors			3,536	3,536	3,536
	Tactic 2: Advertise locally and digitally					
	Tactic 3: Flyer handout					
	Total Expense	0	0	46,408	31,408	31,408
ROI		**0**	**0**	**13,592**	**58,592**	**118,592**

In our example, Pathway 14 has NO incremental expense, and that really changes things (Table 14.3).

Assessing the Outcome

Joe's Coffee illustrates the importance of financials in strategic planning. If you didn't run the numbers, having a live band would make all the sense in the world! By running the numbers at this step we were able not only to identify a problem but also to come up with a solution. There were many other solutions we could have come up with as well: We could have charged a cover to hear the band, we could have found a cheaper band, we could have increased our revenue line to reflect a higher amount for the band nights, etc. The important thing isn't the solution – that has so much to do with the creatures we are and what we like to do competitively. The important thing is the process step allowing us to identify the challenge.

Strategists assess and overcome practical hurdles.

Assessing the outcome of the total model is critical, and we've given you the best yardstick to measure by, right? You remember – back in the first process step when we defined our goals?

We set 2-, 3-, and 5-year goals on revenues AND profitability. Now's the time to dust them off and look at the output of the model. Did we achieve the goal? If not, then we have to think about why. Did we underestimate the amount of revenue we could earn? Did we spend too much on our strategy implementation? Do we NEED all the strategies we came up with by pathway? Are we double counting expenses – that is, do the expenses in one pathway count toward executing another pathway (in our example, Pathway 6 paid for Pathway 14)? This happens quite a bit as you plan out investments.

For Joe's Coffee, we assigned expected costs for people, rent ($2,500/month), cost of goods sold (COGS) (.50/coffee, $1/pastry), utilities ($400/mo.), and marketing by tactic identified ($4,000/year). We had limited start-up costs since Cameron was leasing all the equipment in the store, and the landlord remodeled as part of the rent agreement.

Assess the output—objectively. Don't fall in love with your own brilliance. Be merciless as you evaluate what is must do versus nice to have. Don't confuse cool with right.

We went through all the pain in Step 1 to give you a compass *for just this exercise*! Use it. (See Table 14.4.)

So, how did Cameron do? Some quick-and-dirty modeling shows that while she underperformed on her profitability goal in year 1, she more than makes up for that in subsequent years, and she creates a business that shows a healthy ROI.

What if I told you that this was really a project we did on directed energy weapons for a defense prime selling into the DoD and I just changed the names and tweaked the tactics to reflect a coffee shop instead of a defense customer?

Table 14.4 Growth Pathway Profit Model

Growth Pathway Profit Model

Joe's Coffee Example

	Y1	Y2	Y3	Y4	Y5	Total
6: New customer acquisition						
Pathway Revenue	0	0	18,000	27,000	45,000	
Pathway Expense	0	0	46,408	31,408	31,408	
Pathway Profitability	**0**	**0**	**(28,408)**	**(4,408)**	**13,592**	
8. Classic new account addition						
Pathway Revenue	25,200	54,000	82,800	90,000	108,000	
Pathway Expense	3,536	3,536	3,536	3,536	3,536	
Pathway Profitability	**21,664**	**50,464**	**79,264**	**86,464**	**104,464**	
14. Existing customer product migration						
Pathway Revenue	0	0	42,000	63,000	105,000	
Pathway Expense	0	0	0	0	0	
Pathway Profitability	**0**	**0**	**42,000**	**63,000**	**105,000**	
16. "Milking the cow"						
Pathway Revenue	126,000	126,000	168,000	210,000	210,000	
Rent	30,000	30,000	30,000	30,000	30,000	
Staff	56,000	56,000	56,000	56,000	56,000	
COGS	23,625	23,625	31,500	39,375	39,375	
Marketing	4,000	4,001	4,002	4,003	4,004	
Pathway Expenses	113,625	113,626	121,502	129,378	129,379	
Pathway Profitability	**12,375**	**12,374**	**46,498**	**80,622**	**80,621**	
Gross Revenue	151,200	180,000	310,800	390,000	468,000	1,500,000
Gross Expense	117,161	117,162	171,446	164,322	164,323	734,414
Gross Profit	34,039	62,838	139,354	225,678	303,677	765,586
					ROI	49%

How about if this was for a medical device manufacturer standing up a new type of point-of-care diagnostic? Instead of coffee, they sold machines. Instead of musicians and an open mike, they are going to add new types of assays that will diagnose new disease types in year 3.

This process works for any business.

Iterative Loop

At this point, if you cannot achieve your goal, you have to cycle back to Step 4: Select Growth Pathways. Examine your assumptions and your growth framework. Either reset the assumptions or find the next pathway on the tree that offers you revenues opportunity to achieve goal. Go to Step 5 and create strategies and tactics. Then through Step 6 and run the numbers. Do this until you feel confident that you have reached your goals.

Make no mistake, this is a heavy lift, but it's a really valuable exercise.

Before we go on, let's recap where we are at.

- If you've done this right, you understand the mission and its goals.
- With a fully self-aware mindset, you've come to know the needs and wants of customers and the threats and capabilities of competitors.
- You've been able to build a team of experts in each of the functional areas of your company and had them each contribute from their perspective as you think about your battle planning.
- You've built your plan, being challenged with all the obvious and nuanced challenges that the team could throw at you, and you've solved for them all.
- The Doers are on board, the Vetoers are in line.
- You built out a model to assess in an unbiased, objective way if you can achieve the mission. Through a series of cycles, you have proved you can do it.
- In proving to both yourself and your function-leading teammates that you can grow to the goal, you've created confidence and

buy-in from the very people whom you will need to execute. That is immensely powerful stuff. That is what it takes to achieve your strategy.

Think about how far you've come – from a new practitioner sitting alone trying to figure out what you are supposed to do, to the structured, competent leader with not only a plan but also the capability to succeed. Well done.

There's only one last sanity check to perform and we are through.

15

Map Strategy to a Timeline

Step 7: The Power of a Picture

One of the challenges in as rigorous an exercise as this planning has been is to keep activities aligned at both the highest possible level and also at the lowest. For our purposes and the last step in our process, we literally draw the timing of each action on a Gantt chart.

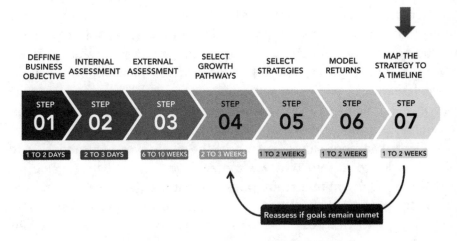

182 GROWING THE TOP LINE

Harmonograms

Harmonograms, more commonly called Gantt charts, were created a long time ago but were made popular in the early 1900s by Henry Gantt. Mr. Gantt's creation was used to help the war effort in WWI. Given the alignment with war planning and game theory that you will find in our model, it only seems fitting that we find continued value in this approach.

When I was a newly minted MBA I worked for a firm called A.T. Kearney. Although I had a relatively short tenure there, I learned to respect the value of a Gantt chart not only for organization but also as a financial tool. Whether I was working to redesign the call centers at FedEx or helping improve the performance of specialty valve manufacturers, it was hammered home to me that we had to be pragmatic and understand the relationship between workstreams and tasks as we thought about helping our clients. This has been proven true time and time again in my career.

There are really two words that I worry about when I teach Beacon's method to growth: *empathy* (which we've already covered) and *pragmatism.*

The primary complaint I hear about consultants as a group is that we offer "pie in the sky" or are "too cerebral." Pragmatism is all about making sure the thinking is capable of the doing. In our process, we have done the thinking. We have climbed the mountain and created a brilliant strategy/tactic pool for our firm to achieve our stated goals. We've tried to inject pragmatism throughout by including multiple functional areas in the strategy design process. We've further been structured in the use of financials in our work. Calculating both expected revenues and costs allows us to win over the investor, finance, and management community of our companies, even if for entrepreneurs that is a community of one.

Gantt charting allows us to add the final layer of practical, critical thought to ensure that we can achieve the goal that we've set ourselves. Our entire set of pathways, strategies, and tactics can be represented on a Gantt chart visually. This will include schedule, resources, and progress. It shows the tasks to be done and when.

Most important, it should show dependency from task to task as well as start and end dates.

This is a critical capability as you wrap up your planning process. If you did this as part of a team, you were managing multiple individuals with conflicting agendas and scorecards. They each had their own biases that have made them good at the jobs they do. They also have very different spans of control/influence in the ongoing business. Its normal for them to worry about their own fiefdom before they worry about the whole. We've taken them out of that comfort zone and had them put on strategy hats. By definition, a strategy forces you to consider all functional perspectives and, most important, the market perspective.

As a group, you were creative and broad thinking. As we worked through the financial model, that creativity was tested against the original aims of the project. We are going to test again, but through a different lens. We will consolidate all tasks under each tactic and each strategy and align them on a single calendar. When you do this, experience says that a few pragmatic issues become immediately apparent.

Overloading the System

When you consolidate tasks at this stage, you quickly realize that there are unrealistic start dates for many of them. Always too early. Remember, unless you are a start-up, you have existing activities underway that you are planning to get a yield from. You typically don't want to disrupt those, and there is a transitional period that is required to both realize the promise of prior efforts and plan ahead for future success. By simply stacking start times simultaneously at the beginning of a planning period you are guaranteed to *overload the system*.

Underestimation of Dependency Time Demands

You have to think through the "dependency" of tasks on one another in the tactical layers of planning. Let's use the example used in Chapter 14 of Joe's Coffee. Cameron wanted to provide incremental revenues through a live music and open-mike night. One of the early tactics we listed was the building of a stage and setup of both microphones and lighting. These are precursor tasks. Absent the existence of a stage with sound and lighting, it's unlikely that the strategy can be executed upon. This is a pretty simple example, but if you look at other leaders we've spoken with, you can imagine the difficulty of estimating "precursor" tasks. Think about the shift from a product company to a services-focused company. When Microsoft 365 was conceived, Microsoft had to first build the technical capability to provide the services, then create a marketing campaign, then the infrastructure to deploy and bill for it, and finally, perhaps the most difficult, they had to socialize the concept, train the sales and support function, and change the accounting/HR systems to accurately represent and incentivize the sales force. When people plan, they are inevitably optimistic. We need to help them be worst case in thought for the execution phase. It's great to have a glass-half-full mentality, but lousy to learn that it's actually half empty and you are scrambling for the pitcher. An overused saying, but it's much better to know how long it will take to fill a new pitcher as you start serving.

Disruption of Existing Initiatives

This is an obvious but very real challenge. In pursuit of the new, do you ignore the old? Too many plans fail to account for the importance of current efforts and prior year planning. When you consider Pathway 16: Milking the Cow or Pathway 14: Existing Customer Product Migration, recognize that executing on that profitability has quite a bit to do with executing on the promises of the past. If our planning process teaches you anything, it's that you don't have to be truly disruptive to your core business to achieve your goals. In fact, if you are disrupting it, you had better be in survival mode, because existing customers will want you to be predictable.

Hiring Needs

There is nothing more eye opening than sitting down with your HR/recruiting staff and telling them that you need new resources to achieve a new strategy. Depending on your relationship with those leaders, you will either get cursed at or laughed at. Very rarely is it a positive response (although COVID is creating a new market environment on this one for a VERY short time – see Chapter 16). You have to respect the challenge of resourcing. Strategies and tactics ultimately boil down to people, and if you get the people wrong, well, woe unto you. If you have the wrong team, you are screwed (I may have paraphrased Tom Lantzsch of Intel here). Finding the right people is a hard and underappreciated task. It's like the people at B-School who look back 20 years later and say "Wow – wish I had paid more attention in OB [organizational behavior]," and then realize that they really meant getting the right people into the team. That's all HR, the underfunded, unsung hero of operations.

Flawed Financial Modeling

This is an intellectual way of saying that we don't have the budget. While you might be able to afford the aggregated costs of a strategy, cash flow is everything – especially for a smaller company. Having an awareness of when things happen, the dependencies that they have, and their resulting costs is often eye opening when considered in the aggregate. The Gantt chart helps you understand this.

Creating a Gantt chart can be a high-level or very detailed process. You can literally be certified in the tool as a project manager in different circles. Both Six Sigma and PMP certification require a working skill with Gantts and for good reason. So many software tools exist to facilitate Gantt charting that I'm not going to recommend one or spend too much time on this. It's most important that you know what you get from going through the mapping drill.

Gantt charts let you do two very distinct things. They demonstrate interdependencies and track progress. A very high-level example can be seen in Figure 15.1.

Gantt charts don't need to be overly complex. We want to be able to show the entire strategy and its timing in a single picture. I've had some clients who put financials directly on this – the cost and revenues associated with strategies and tactics –but I don't think you need to

FOR SELECTED PATHWAYS, MAP THE STRATEGY OVER A TIMELINE

Recognize that strategy will include a number of pathways, and there may be synergies or challenges when combined

07 ▸ **MAP STRATEGIES AND TACTICS ALONG A TIMELINE**

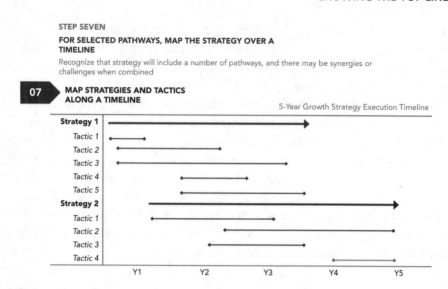

FIGURE 15.1   Gantt Chart Mapping Strategies and Tactics along a Timeline

do that. Most important in this step is the gut reaction of the team as they see the whole. Up to this point they may have been a bit siloed in their thinking. This construct shows the whole project in a single view and makes those earlier issues quite obvious. When the Doer functions see this picture, they will throw flags like a referee at a Tampa Bay/Chiefs Superbowl! "We don't have the people!" "We don't have the budget!" "No way we meet that deadline" – you will hear it all, and your challenge is to separate wheat from chaff. What's sandbagging, what is real? That's a judgment call for you to make, but you HAVE to listen to it all and ideally document it for discussion. Part of our job in this exercise is to win over the Doer function by being pragmatic and empathetic. If someone who has been involved in the creation of the plan is now calling a foul, then you need to stop and listen. Ignore the disagreement at your own peril. Smart strategists will listen, challenge, judge, and incorporate.

The incorporation step is what you care about from a process standpoint, and any decision you make needs to involve the finance team member. The reality of shifting a timeline – moving it to allow for the development of a product, the hiring of new employees, the fruition of a prior plan – forces the economics to change.

Since we are at a strategy level, it's likely that the changes we see are material and impact revenue and expense models. By engaging finance we are able to determine what, if any, effect the changes will have on our ability to achieve the goal from both a revenue and cost perspective.

It's incredibly important that you run the numbers and see if you underperform target. If so, you have to go back to Step 4 to either increase the revenue lines associated with the offending pathways or consider adding new pathways that add to the financial performance of the team.

Once You Complete This Step, You Have Finished!

You now have the following:

1. A clear statement of mission/objective
   a. Financial
   b. Timing
   c. Strategic
2. An unbiased understanding of capability, resourcing, and culturally acceptable behaviors in achieving target
3. A full understanding of the market condition – customers, competitors, and regulatory agencies
4. An exhaustive mapping of potential growth pathways, with an understanding of gross, annual, and pathway-driven revenue planning
5. An ROI-driven set of growth strategies and tactics
6. A pragmatic assessment of timing associated with tasks
7. An engaged and committed leadership team across ALL functional areas of the company

Congratulations! That's it. That's what it takes to plan a growth strategy, except, now there is the doing.

It's funny – every once in a while, I have a client ask me to sign up for performance-based contracting. That is, "Hey, Cliff, how about you do this project and I'll give you a percentage of revenues." This is a TOTALLY reasonable ask from their perspective. Why in the world would they engage in a strategy that the consultant wouldn't sign up for?

However, I will NEVER sign up for this unless we are hired and *empowered* to execute the strategy ourselves, and even then it will have a 200% to 300% performance kicker on the original project cost. I'm not being greedy, I'm being pragmatic and managing risk. Instead, we put a performance guarantee on ALL our work product, and have since I founded the firm over 20 years ago. Half of our project fee is fully at risk based on client satisfaction. We invite our clients to pay to their level of satisfaction. On over 1,500 projects, there are fewer than a handful of clients who haven't paid their bill in full, and that is typically because we weren't satisfied with the product we provided and withheld our final invoice.

Remember when we started this book I made the statement about those who can and those who can't? If you've read to this point, you should know that I'm not kidding. Executing a strategy is a force of will. Our process to this point has been to align your team with your intent. To harness their thought and pre-engineer out their objections. To get them committed to the goal as a pragmatic, achievable exercise. We have upped the probability of success significantly. In fact, the reason that Beacon has delivered over 1,500 projects with over 90% repeat customers is because of the effectiveness of our approach.

Execution is simply hard. The people that I interviewed for this book are all an amazing blend of Thinker and Doer. Scientist and Mac-Gyver. Coach and player. They can conceive of a plan and then success-fully act on it, and I've tried to pass along some of their accumulated wisdom.

Executing on a growth strategy is setting course on an open ocean. Even with a seaworthy boat and a crack crew, challenges arise, hurdles are faced, and resolve is tested. Sometimes it is sweet, sweet sail-ing – the water is calm, the breeze is steady, and the course is clear. Sometimes it is a storm, the seas are in chaos, and the crew is sick or in mutiny. As a professional I've faced that particular challenge three times: post 9/11, 2008, and right now, in the days of COVID.

16

Navigating in a Storm: Growth in a COVID World

My original proposal for this book in February 2020 didn't mention anything about COVID-19. This book was written to help all companies consider how to grow, but the situation we are now living through requires thoughtful consideration from a growth strategist's perspective.

The pandemic is a storm.

It was a fast-approaching, highly underestimated storm that in hindsight seems incomprehensible. Not to epidemiologists who had been predicting an event like this for years, but to business thinkers.

As I write this book, vaccines are being deployed and the science looks good, so I'm optimistic. However, after every major storm, there is damage, clean-up, and rebuilding. This will take years, so I wanted to add a chapter on employing growth strategy at a time like this.

The framework still applies (see Figure 16.1).

FIGURE 16.1 The Full Growth Strategy Framework

Step 1: What are your goals and how has COVID changed them?

Step 2: How has COVID honestly impacted your organization and shown its strengths and weaknesses?

Step 3: What impact has COVID had on political, economic, customer, and competitor market variables?

Step 4: How do we apply these new realities to the framework?

Step 5: What are the resulting strategies and tactics by pathway?

Step 6: Will the post-COVID environment support the economics of our plan?

Step 7: How does timing play out given new external behaviors?

As you apply this process, being frank about your situation is imperative. Companies fall into one of three categories during the pandemic – those who are drowning, those who are ducking waves, and those who are choosing to surf. Make no mistake, your company is in one (or all) of these three modes. By knowing where you are, you can make smart business decisions.

John Beering talked about the unexpected challenges of COVID to his business. The best of the best are honest with themselves, and John was fast to understand the challenges they faced:

COVID is another good example. Spending two thirds of your time focused on how you are going to make payroll. How am I going to stay cash positive? That's why growth had to mostly go on hold.

It was survival mode because we didn't know what we were getting into next. Having a process and a discipline around keeping that in focus is important.

Don't bite off more than you can chew. What's good about your framework is as an organization, and as an individual, we can really focus well on three or four things max. What are those three or four things that we're going to focus on that are the needle-moving items for future? In my context I'm merging four businesses. I'm just trying to survive COVID. I've gotta take care of customers in a compassionate way each and every day.

They won't teach you this in B-School, and it is meaningful as you consider why we weren't better prepared as businesses to cope with COVID. Think of it as "willful denial." That is, corporate creatures know there is a risk, but don't believe it will happen to them. Companies do math to predict what could be, but spend to respond to what is. Politicians agreed there was a threat, but without an "adverse event" it would be impossible to get funding.

You have to be savvy as you chart your course through the pandemic and think in terms of short, medium, and long term according to Tom Lantzsch of Intel:

Clearly it's [COVID] accelerating the use of these technologies on a global scale. We can interact with our customers and ourselves in ways that we didn't think were possible, that we thought were dictated by airplanes. It's fundamentally changing that, and I think a lot of companies are investing their capital assets in that right now. I think that's short term, and that's not where I play.

Tom's right here. Where we used to get on a plane to meet with customers, we are now doing it via Zoom, Skype, and Teams. Every company in the enterprise, education, healthcare, and retail domains has made significant investment in this area. He went on:

Medium and longer term I'm really spending my time considering how people operate things in a world where they can't physically be there . . . we're doing demonstrations on ourselves . . . Oscilloscopes and logic analyzers and all these things. How do you deal with the world where you can't put people in there.

Tom has identified a new market need driven by the challenges of COVID. Not how employees collaborate, but how can they operate a physical environment remotely.

> And, by the way, we're reinventing ourselves. It's awesome where we are now creating ways where our engineers can collaborate on the same product in five different time zones. We're creating what we call remote access labs to go do that . . . Now we're integrating things like robotics and artificial with virtual reality, so literally you could sit at your desk and drive a robot to probe a board like you are in an Intel Lab. That to me is no different than a patient sitting in a hospital. It's the same problem? It's a room. My patient is a "board." It's got gear hooked up to it. In my world, it's oscilloscope. It could be an EKG machine and a surgeon can be any place on the planet, and we are overlaying all this technology. In our world it would be a schematic of a board, but in a surgeon's world it could be the X Ray or an MRI right on top of the patient, so they're looking at MRI on top of the patient real-time remotely.

Tom's example shows that COVID isn't only a destroyer, it is a market creator and accelerator. I'm not sure where your opportunities are as you read this, but there will be an opportunity to rebound and take advantage of the post-COVID reconstruction period. Let's talk about how to succeed at this by looking at some rules Beacon has observed emerging in real time.

Your Existing Assumptions Are Likely Wrong

There is nothing worse for a consultant than to learn that their work is no good. This happened across the client base that we serve as 2020 progressed. We either over- or underestimated the rates of growth versus prior years due to the COVID crisis. All those brilliant 5-year market sizings we did – scrap 'em. They aren't any good for you to make business decisions from. Can you imagine the difficulty you have as a vendor when you have to tell your best customers that their spend with you last year is moot? But it's a truth. Honest self- and market awareness is critical to surviving the COVID story. If you are in healthcare, you were either a winner or a loser for the first 6 months of COVID as hospitals dealt with the pandemic, pharma searched for a cure, Centers for Medicare and Medicaid Services (CMS) guidelines relaxed to allow remote care reimbursement, and elective surgeries were frozen. If you were in the tech sector, you were either a winner or a loser as the markets shifted to support work from home, educate from home, and care from home. Manufacturers pivoted to produce masks, ventilators, and hand sanitizer. Videos and gaming enjoyed unexpected growth, and brick-and-mortar retail hit the skids. Recognizing that things are now fundamentally different than a year ago is critical.

You Probably Don't Know How to Talk to Your Customer Anymore

It's not your fault. Customers just can't meet with you the way that they did before. No more firm handshakes in corporate lobbies, two-hour luncheons, fist bumps at conventions, weekly check-ins . . . COVID has thrown a wrench into all that. We actually spend quite a bit of time helping our clients think though this new world order of engagement, content, and cadence. How often do people want to meet with you? What do they want to talk to you about? Video? Text? Call? Everything is in flux across every industry. However you talked to your clients before is simply wrong right now.

PRO TIP

Sue Spradley
CEO, Motion Intelligence; Board of Directors, Avaya and Qorvo Corporations

A little humility goes a long way in learning how to create a strategy, because when you're humble in your listening, and then you think and speak, 99% of the time people will say, "Oh, wow, that's really valuable. I learned something from that today. I want to run with that."

Sue Spradley talked about how the pandemic was impacting her marketing activity. You remember Sue from Chapter 13, but she didn't talk about what her new start-up does. Motion Intelligence is a company that is taking on distracted driving for fleet operators and individual drivers. They are a group of seasoned industry professionals deploying amazing tech to make the roads safer and more for entities around the world. She talked about how her traditional approach to sales has had to change:

> As an entrepreneur, we're now going through this thing called the COVID pandemic. Where you would traditionally put four or five people on the road in a car, in a plane, say "go meet," those days are done. We can no longer just go to trade shows, so you really learn how to do some of these new account additions through using online tools like LinkedIn. They have become so much more important than they were 6 months ago. We have grown and have more customers engage. Now, partially, I think because our team has had to learn how to stay extremely focused because they now have to go get everybody on a zoom call and for our business, they have to convince somebody how a device that goes in a vehicle works . . . by video! It's a very different sales approach.

She's absolutely right – traditional means don't work right now so you have to adapt your approach to be effective.

Supply Chains Are Suffering

Every industry is impacted by this underappreciated and misunderstood functional area. The biggest initial issue is trade policy between nations. The Trump Administration has been forcing the China trade issue for quite some time. In fact, we threw a flag on this for our clients well before things escalated to the current state. So, raw materials are disrupted, manufacturing is disrupted as companies defend against the disease, and shipping lags as there is a major increase in e-commerce activities. The perfect storm is disrupted supply chains that have a cascading effect on your ability to meet your customers' expectations.

It's a Buyers' Market

If you think back to Q3 of 2019, the US had ~3.5% unemployment. You couldn't find a good person to hire! HR was pulling its hair out trying to meet the needs of businesses.

Then COVID hit, and the US had over 20 million unemployed in very, very short order. Companies went extinct in a blink. Layoffs happened as leaders realized they were facing an existential threat. A glut of talent sat on the bench, and no one had faith that a recovery would be any time soon.

Here's a stunning fact: 18 of our 50 states (that's 36% of our states) had both record low unemployment and record high unemployment in 2020. Chew on that for a second. According to the Bureau of Labor Statistics, it's true – and I only had data through August 2020! Nevada reported a record low of 3.6% unemployment in February 2020. In April, two short months later, they reported a record high unemployment of a whopping 30.1%! If you needed proof of the severity of the economic storm of COVID, there it is.

Once a viable treatment for COVID is deployed we are right back into the people crisis. Savvy companies recognize this truth, and right now, it's a buyers' market, as companies of scale exercise their inorganic growth muscles not just for revenues or IP, but for the people that acquisitions bring, knowing they will be needed when they factor in the 3- and 5-year horizons that we as growth strategy consultants recommend.

Revenue Opportunity Will Align with Government Investment

The cardiac system of the global economy market is in arrythmia. That means that things are either moving too fast or too slow versus the normal cadence we have established over time. Tachycardia/bradycardia . . . neither is great as both are unanticipated and damaging if unchecked. As an economist I'm pretty comfortable with assessing the valuable lessons that history has to teach. The Great Depression was a staggering blow to us, not due to physical health but due to economic loss (that led to physical decline). There is literally no example in living history that we can refer to that will help us understand the current COVID crisis more than the Great Depression. I grew up to stories of the Great Depression from my dad. He was a pretty sharp character and did the job that every father hopes to do for their children well. He taught me how to fend for myself by explaining how the world worked. He was an Army Air Corps WWII veteran who had been shot down early in the war and spent over three years in a German prison camp. He talked a lot about what led up to the war and the role of the government driving recovery. The New Deal. The Tennessee Valley Authority. The creation of the SEC. It was compelling stuff for a kid who turned into an economist and strategist, and I soaked up his wonderful blend of sociopolitical insight, along with his practical nature. I can almost hear his voice today – "The government will have to invest to drive a recovery. It won't matter the political party; we've been hit and hit hard. Pay attention to what they are up to . . ."

So, if you look, you'll see around the world that there are massive infrastructure build-outs planned. Some traditional, some not. 5G infrastructure build-out, the deregulation of healthcare, the availability of 6 GHz spectrum, mandates for high-speed access, investment in online and hybrid education, road infrastructure, incentives for solar, smart cities . . . the list is pretty large. Billions are being spent to help the global economy recover. Study it, engage at the right spots, and grow.

Successful Growth Becomes a Relative Metric

Those truths are the "inside baseball" realities of doing business right now. While this book is about growth, not all industries are capable of growing right now, so *growth becomes a relative metric.* This is a really important point, so let me tell a story to explain it a bit more.

When I first started sailing, I was older. I worked for Oracle, and ran their Northeast Communications services practice. My clients were

AT&T, Cablevision, and the 222 subsidiary companies of Time, Inc. I lived in Boston and took the Delta shuttle to an office in Manhattan. Living La Vida.

Delta gave away free magazines at the shuttle, and one was a sailing magazine. I fell in love with the stories I read, and then dreamed of the life of a sailor while tethered firmly to my desk. My wife suggested we get a sailboat one summer and we were hooked.

I'm pretty competitive, so inevitably I started to race. We raced in the small but urban city of Portsmouth, New Hampshire, about an hour north of Boston on the New Hampshire seacoast. What a great group of welcoming and tolerant sailors!

We raced at the mouth of the Piscataqua River, which is a natural barrier that separates New Hampshire from Maine. The Piscataqua (unbeknownst to me at the time) is the third fastest navigable river in the US. It runs over 4 knots in either direction twice a day due to the tides. That means that the current in the river is extreme, a fact well known to all the people who had grown up racing there. I unfortunately didn't get this memo in my short sailing career.

The day of my first race our boat was perfect. She was freshly washed and waxed. Sails were crisp. Bottom had been scrubbed and the crew was looking good. We were ready. It was a light air day with a variable wind predicted, and we got out to the course a bit late because we hadn't anticipated how long the sail to get to the starting line would take.

With a minute to go before the start, the wind shut off. In sailing, like business, you need a currency to make you go, and in sailing the wind is the money. There's nothing worse in sailing than being "in a hole." The sails flog, you get panicky, tempers flare. It's pretty bad. But then it got worse. We realized that the current, much like the economy we all operate in today, was running against us in such a powerful way it was literally pulling us away from the starting line!

I had never experienced anything like this before. We couldn't make headway to the starting line. We were pointing forwards but sailing backwards! How was this possible? I know this is the feeling many business owners and leaders feel today. You are doing everything right, working hard, and yet you can't get ahead.

When I looked around at the other boats, I saw that about half the fleet had thrown out their anchors. Their sails were luffing in the wind, but they weren't going backwards. My sails were pulling, but I was falling far behind. I couldn't even make the starting line in my first race.

While I learned a lot in that race, I mostly learned that success is relative and dependent on the environment. I couldn't control that river any more than you can control the economy. You have to accept the new rules of the game and adapt. The sailors who threw out their anchors were brilliant. They didn't get ahead of the river, but they beat the hell out of me. They were creative and adapted to their situation. This is a winning mindset for strategists in the time of COVID-19.

Quite a few businesses have thrown out an anchor, riding out the political, economic, societal storms we've been living in through the time of this writing. They are waiting out calmer waters. It has been declared that Biden has won, there are viable vaccines authorized for emergency use, economies are starting to recover, but COVID rates continue to rise at unprecedented levels as more than one American dies per minute due to COVID, and that rate is forecasted to double in the coming days.[2] It's still an uncertain domain, but I'm excited by the recovery I know is around the corner.

I think there are a few trends that are here to stay that you need to factor in with your post-COVID growth planning.

Work from Home

With the exception of those deemed an "essential business" chances are you are working from home. Most employers aren't yet willing to absorb the risk of mandating a full-time presence in the office. Work-from-home has massive implications for companies who either served the office setting or are enabling the environment of work-from-home. Consider the practical implications of a remote workforce. The cultural reluctance of a team working from home no longer exists. For a short time after 9/11 there was a general consensus in the tech industry that we would see a major shift toward videoconferencing solutions facilitating corporate and client communications. But it didn't happen as expected for a number of reasons (most of them technical), but once public confidence was restored, we went back to our old practices. It's unclear whether we will do that in the future.

We expected and saw a near-term swing toward production to meet immediate network and storage capacity increase requirements, quickly followed by innovation in the software layer as companies develop new and powerful ways to harness productivity from a reconfigured workforce. This will truly be an "edge" environment, with home infrastructure serving more workload challenges as the compute and storage environment handles work, school, gaming, telehealth, and shopping at an unprecedented degree.

- We will emerge from the current crisis with a much higher percentage of ongoing remote workforce interactions.
- Network capacity will require build-out in the near term to support higher levels of video-based streamed collaboration, requiring a significant focus on home/edge environments.
- Current videoconferencing solutions are sufficient to facilitate most collaboration services, but new methods/processes will be used to facilitate work.
- A new form of relationship, largely in line with other types of online social interactions, will emerge between customer and provider across domains. Generationally this will have the most impact on older employees, as millennials currently communicate mostly through nonverbal chat/social environments and they will lead in the creation of workflows.
- New management techniques will be required to encourage productivity from staff unaccustomed or ill-equipped to work from home. New tools/techniques/processes will be required for this.
- A redefinition of "community" and how we interact is underway. This is especially true in the office and enterprise world. How we build and maintain relationships is going to be amazing to watch.
- Telehealth will be the standard primary point of care for many in the world, and the role of self-service kiosks will continue to grow.

Educate from Home

Almost independent of age, students are experiencing a hybrid or education-from-home model. K–12 is a particularly challenging group since most parents consider this a form of childcare, and COVID makes childcare risky. High schools are working toward normalcy, but with massive COVID rates emerging there, the jury is out on how the rest of the 2020–2021 school year will end up. Universities are struggling to keep educating with a student body that is fully aware of the risks of education during the pandemic, with many electing to have remote or hybrid courses for students. What kinds of opportunities exist here? Chromebooks have dominated the market as a low-cost standard for school systems to provide to their students. Wi-Fi routers and modem vendors have struggled to meet demand for higher speed access as students taking classes compete with working parents who are also online. *Zoom* is now a household word. There are sizeable opportunities to chase here.

Remote Healthcare

CMS controls Medicare and Medicaid reimbursement policy, which has historically driven the practices of private insurers in the US and globally. On December 1, 2020, CMS announced the Trump Administration finalized permanent expansion of Medicare telehealth services.[3] This is a revolutionary change.

Over 20 years ago I did my first project in telehealth for a large Canadian telecom provider. Their value proposition was eerily consistent with how we talk about the value of remote care today. This concept is not new! What's different is that now, for the first time, we are encouraging the use of telehealth ecosystems to treat patients, and companies are focusing on how to drive the scaling of this market. What's amazing and intriguing is that companies are aware of the potential to do something entirely new and new markets are being created. New devices, the deployment of artificial intelligence, the collision of social media and behavioral data are being mixed together not just to meet the standard of care that we've had in doctors' offices historically, but to IMPROVE it! Why limit yourself to what was?

Tom Lantzsch, SVP and GM IoT Group at Intel Corporation:

> What it's doing is accelerating things. I mean I'm doubling down on healthcare right now, where I probably wouldn't have been a year and a half ago. Specifically I'm focused on AI because to make these great models, you have to have data. And in healthcare, historically due to privacy reasons, there were a lot of stovepipes of data and not a lot of sharing. We're doing some new cool technology called Federated Learning that keeps it separate. So you don't know where the data sources but we can get access to these big data pools and apply some really cool AI to it. I think it's going to be great for humankind. I think countries are going to be more participatory in that. We can solve a lot of really tough problems in the world if we collaborate a little bit more.

The New New of Food Service

Six-foot distancing, mandatory shutdowns of bars and restaurants, and a slow recovery have forced many restaurants out of business. Those who have survived have transitioned to the "new new." Food delivery. Half-capacity. Parking lots converted to outdoor seating. Contactless service. The nature of growth says that not everything is dying, even within a suffering industry. Know what did well throughout the pandemic in food service? Bet you bought some . . . pizza! Drive-throughs generally fared better than eat-ins. The reality is restaurants are a really tough business with margins in the single digits. The pandemic has forced companies to adapt to exist and for some to thrive. One interesting dynamic that emerged was the move many restaurants made to create a market for staples during shortages. If their local regulatory system allowed, people could buy pantry staples for themselves at restaurants using their commercial supply chains during times of scarcity in traditional supermarkets. Delivery, curbside pickup, digital promotions – all have become standard.

But as innovative as restaurants are, they are facing some of the worst of this storm. They have to throw out their anchor and fight just to survive. As strategists, when recovery does come to the industry – and it will come – existing customers will be the single most important part of the revenue streams as locals and regulars venture out to resume the lives that we've lost. Unfortunately, survival is the best that most restaurants can hope for in the "new new."

Planning for the Recovery

So, how do you plan for the post-COVID recovery? There are some clear rules you should consider.

Follow the Money

While markets are constricting or beginning to recover right now, there are areas within every market that are more likely to spend than others. The primary aims of any organization seeking growth should be to identify, plan for, and penetrate these opportunities. Organizations MUST challenge long-held assumptions about market opportunity and focus and ensure that they are in "good breeze" relative to their competitors.

Lower Overhead

Operations Management 101: Sounds simple, but it's very important. Do a line-by-line review of your costs and assess as "must have," "nice to have," and "not-necessary." Cut hard, but be strategic. For example, if you know you are going to invest in BD resources in a currently under-performing area, don't hamstring yourself by cutting your production capability in that area. If you've done this already, great. But look at it hard again if it's been more than 6 months since your exercise. Change is constant in this world.

Increase Sales Effort

It is necessary to manage costs, and it is also important to invest in expanding your BD footprint. For smaller firms, focus on selling more things (new or old) to existing clients (most efficient). For larger firms, use your compensation plan to drive broader coverage of markets. You need to cast a wider net to make up for the decline in opportunities in a down market.

Lower Price to Win Business

Rather than worrying strictly about top-line growth, worry about keeping the business running. Much better to decrease sales price by 10% to win work that keeps employees busy than to toe the hard line and lose large chunks of work. Rather than shutting down a factory or laying off workers, take less margin on a sale to keep production rolling.

Be Responsive, Not Panicked

When you are responding to a change in the market environment, involve your entire team and move in unison. Lack of clarity on the why and how of change can lead to sloppy execution and a resulting negative effect on the business.

Bottom-Up Assessments = Tactical Health

Pipeline reviews are the single most useful tool to determine both the near-term financial health (aka boat speed) as well as the fit of the offering with the wants/needs of the market (sail trim). If pipeline has low probability opportunities, dig into why they are low: If no budget, then you are focused in the wrong markets; if a poor fit, then change the value proposition. This is the best near-term sensing device you have.

Assess Org Structure and Staffing Levels

Look at your business at three levels – sales force, managers, Doers. Are you resourced correctly at each level by headcount? Dollars spent? Forecast work based on the earlier pipeline review and expected investments in sales force – all else flows from that. Align your resources accordingly.

Target Competitors for Share Grab

In declining markets, there is always the opportunity to grow by taking share away from your competitors. Choose strategic targets that you can win against and focus scarce resources/attention on them.

Maintain Focus and Morale

People need to believe that there is always a chance to win (simply because there is). In down economies, unpredictable opportunities will arise, and making sure that you keep the core team happy, engaged, motivated, and focused on these opportunities will help you succeed. Invest in letting your team know that you are committed to them no matter what.

Go Where Others Aren't

Key to survival in down economies is identification of whitespace: areas with little/no competition or where your value proposition is a significant differentiator. Make sure that if you are focusing on a market with stiff competition, you believe that market represents your best take away opportunity.

Understand the Market

Far too often in a down economy, companies focus on cost to the exclusion of all else. Cost is critical, and should be addressed, but it is always a finite game. You can only cut to zero. Growth is needed once you can't cut any lower. It is imperative for companies to identify revenue opportunities. Income expansion is at the very least as important as cost management, for without revenue, cost simply doesn't matter. So, study the markets to learn where the opportunity is. Find your breeze and sail to victory.

Take Calculated Risks

While you want to stick to fundamentals, you have to be willing to take an educated risk if you believe there is valid market opportunity.

Winning tactics include investing in adjacent markets or in a disruptive technology with a near-term payoff. Make sure, though, that you understand and can survive the risk. Only in very dire situations would you take a risk that could put the company in peril.

I hope these rules help. For those of you interested in how they apply to sailing, check out the whitepaper "Racing in Light Air" at www.beacongroupconsulting.com.

The challenges of COVID illustrate how to plan if you are in the role of driving growth in a struggling business. For many, the challenge is simply survival. However, you could also be in a situation where everything is going well, demand is strong, and you can't keep up with it. The industries we see that happening in relate to things like communications infrastructure, telemedicine, groceries, liquor stores, delivery services, gaming, streaming, and social media.

These high-growth industries have the inverse problem – too much demand! This is a really dangerous condition for a growth strategist, because you think you don't have to be strategic, you just have to fulfill demand. I can't tell you how many calls I had in the first half of 2020 with people in networking or healthcare-focused roles who "didn't need help" because business was too good.

Here's the peril – you become so tactical in thought, and so self-assured of success that you miscue on duration and environmental factors. Remember that business is a battle fought on a terrain against opponents. Right now, every one of the companies who have experienced success and unprecedented demand need to be thinking strategically about how to sustain it. Let's look at telemedicine.

A huge question exists in whether or not the reimbursement by CMS we talked about previously will continue after the pandemic. Will CMS continue to reimburse the same for an online visit versus an in-office visit, and will patients grow comfortable with the online care environment? Personally, I hope so. However, it's got to be an outcome that companies work to sustain. There are many factors that will fight against this. Human nature is factor number 1. We have grown up used to being cared for by a person, in person. Can we let that go? Another factor is that if we move to an online care environment, that will put a significant amount of financial pressure on the healthcare entities that have invested in the large footprints of medical facilities. Will they lobby the government for a return to normalcy, or will they embrace the efficiencies of remote care? Finally, how quickly will companies of scale invest to support this new form of healthcare? New diagnostic devices, fulfillment capabilities, and billing systems need to emerge to sustain the rapid and potential value of this new ecosystem.

It's really, really easy right now to have hubris if you are in an over-performing sector. If you are building up capacity to meet an abnormal demand: beware. History is littered with companies that overextended to meet the requirements of an abnormal bubble. This pandemic is going to be a factor only until a viable, trusted vaccine is deployed and then there will be a built-up demand for life to go back to normal.

Ever hear of the company Elco? No? Elco stands for Electric Launch Company, which built high-end launches and then larger yachts for the world's elite. Founded in 1899, they built boats for people like John Jacob Astor (who owned four), Grand Duke Alexander of Russia, Henry Ford, Thomas Edison, and Charles Lindbergh. Then World War II hit, and the US Government asked Elco to manufacture PT boats. Elco ramped up manufacturing to build 399 PT boats. They built one every 60 hours, including the famed PT109 for John F. Kennedy. Based in Bay-onne, New Jersey, right by the Statue of Liberty, Elco helped the US win the war.

When the war ended, the massive factory capacity was suddenly not needed. The "bubble" – the anomaly of demand that the war effort created – was simply no more. In 1949, after valiantly attempting to enter a number of different markets, Elco was closed.

Companies doing well today need to be aware of the sustainabil-ity and mortality of their success and have a pragmatic eye toward the end of the pandemic. Much like the dilemma Elco faced, you have to ask yourself, What moves should you make now to prevent the chal-lenge of overcapacity in the event of a return to behaviors that echo pre-pandemic times?

Applying These Rules with the Framework

When you think about the practical application of these rules to our Four Key Questions, it is incredibly clarifying.

Which customers? We shifted even more focus to existing customers during this time frame. Why? They knew and trusted us and gave us much more insight into their budgets and timing (follow the money). We increased our reach-outs (increase sales effort), canvassed our client base broadly to identify those with project work (know your market), and helped those who were transitioning roles due to employers shrinking their workforce (their employers were assessing org structure and workforce). We acquired several new customers as the clients we helped moved to new companies and asked us to serve them there (take calculated risks). Because we are a 20-year-old business, we have a fairly broad client base and were able to focus on those customers that we knew had money. In addition, because we paid attention to those clients during the pandemic, they gave us the inside track on sole-source engagements (go where the others aren't). We also sought clients who we knew needed help but typically worked with more expensive brands (take away share). So for us, we shifted to 95% existing customers.

Geographies we served didn't shift, so it stayed at 100%, but we focused on employee safety and morale, and shifted to a 100% work-from-home structure, with total flexibility for people to head back to their family homes if they chose to. We even had one consultant move to the beach in Puerto Rico for quality of life during the pandemic!

We stayed focused on existing goods and services but added a new practice area to our firm that split out the work we do supporting mergers and acquisitions, which was a calculated risk on our part. The actual work is the same, but we are marketing and accounting for it differently, so the perception is that it's something new.

Our business model didn't change. There was no need for us to do any major shifts in pricing, other than to lower price when necessary to keep the firm busy. Many competitors were so overstaffed that they gave work away free to keep employees busy, which is not a sustainable model. We aligned staffing with business needs, which allowed us to stay economically sound through the darkest of days.

In framework terms, Beacon's pandemic framework looked something like Figure 16.2 during year 1.

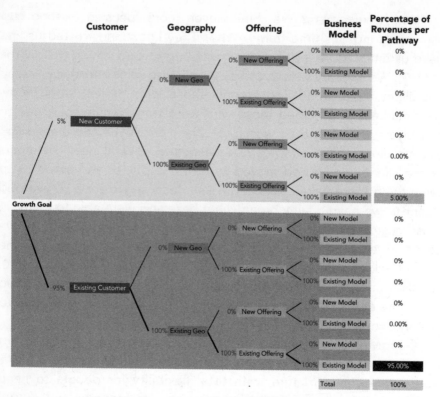

FIGURE 16.2 Beacon's Pandemic Framework

This may surprise you, but after that entire thought process, it became clear to us that there were only two pathways we should be focused on. We focused on our core, low-risk behaviors (Pathway 16 is the lowest risk for any company) and worked to add new accounts where we could pick them up with little exposure/risk. We were able to stay focused on our strengths and we minimized our weaknesses.

By using our process, we've been able to survive the pandemic. While we didn't hit the goals we set at the beginning of the year, we've done better than most of our competitors, which is how we are measuring growth during the pandemic. Our boat is firmly anchored and in the building breeze while many of our competitors are being swept downriver by the current/challenges of the pandemic.

This approach doesn't work for every company. We have clients who are taking advantage of their cash position and scale to acquire as many companies as we can help them identify, because they see this as an opportunity to get good people and intellectual property at a bargain. Others are pushing aggressively into new markets and services as they use the market flux as a repositioning tool. Still others are pursuing geographic expansion as a way to find incremental customers as their traditional markets are drying up. Every company is different, which is why the process steps we've outlined in the book are so critical as you think about growth.

Notes

1. Prudential, "The Cut: Exploring Financial Wellness within Diverse Populations," 2010, http://news.prudential.com/content/1209/files/PrudentialTheCutExploringFinancialWellnessWithinDiversePopulations.pdf?utm_source=businesswire™utm_medium=newsrelease™utm_campaign=thecut.

2. Christina Maxouris, "US Is 'Rounding the Corner into a Calamity,' Expert Says, with Covid-19 deaths Projected to Double," CNN Health, November 28, 2020, https://www.cnn.com/2020/11/28/health/us-coronavirus-saturday/index.html.

3. Centers for Medicare & Medicaid Services, "Trump Administration Finalizes Permanent Expansion of Medicare Telehealth Services and Improved Payment for Time Doctors Spend with Patients," CMS.gov, December 1, 2020, https://www.cms.gov/newsroom/press-releases/trump-administration-finalizes-permanent-expansion-medicare-telehealth-services-and-improved-payment.

Conclusion

It's quite a journey we have been on together.

- We've considered the importance of goal setting and team construct.
- We've learned the kind of creatures we are.
- We've understood how to determine the market and competitive landscape.
- We've thought through the Four Key Questions and how they develop into the 16 Growth Pathways.
- We've planned for growth through applied strategies and tactics.
- We've tied revenue performance to associated costs.
- We've made sure that we can support the timing of these exercises in aggregate.
- Finally, we've considered the unique implications of the COVID-19 crisis and its associated set of strategies for survival.

I appreciate you making the effort to get to this point in the book. I know that business books can be dry, and sometimes they are things you read because you are forced to for work. I hope you picked up this book to help you learn how the best of the best think about growth strategy and its development. There is a pragmatic, effective way to do it, and I've shared an approach that is based on a lifetime of learning. Know that each of the stories, leaders, anecdotes, and methods I've offered are exactly that – an offering to the next generation of practitioner. All of those leaders who contributed to this book have scars . . .

and as good as the tales they have shared are, and as valuable as they are for you to consider, you still must execute!

I started sailing late in life and immersed myself in the sport. I won a North American Championship and became a high school coach and a US sailing instructor. There is nothing more exciting as a coach than to meet people eager to learn. I always start teaching someone how to sail in the classroom. Explain how things work, why boats move through the water, what to do in an emergency, how to go fast, how to stop – how to compete and how to win.

All this learning is great, but it's *intellectual* knowledge (understanding how a thing works), not *experiential* knowledge (lessons learned from the doing of things). At some point, all sailors climb into a boat and immediately understand why a boat is often described as alive when you feel it move beneath your feet. All the kids I coached eventually took a breath, raised the sails, untied the lines, and did what I taught them. They are all good sailors because they have been taught good fundamentals.

You have just been taught really good fundamentals for the development of growth strategy in a variety of conditions. You intellectually understand the process. Now you have to do it for yourself, and I hope that you trust me when I tell you that what we've covered really works. Raise your sails, cast off your lines, and let the breeze carry you on your growth adventure.

I'm here to help if you need it. Just drop me a line at cfarrah@beacongroupconsulting.com and I'll do my best to answer your questions.

December 2020
Destin, FL

Acknowledgments

My first run-in with book publishing was in 1990 when, as a newly minted consultant, I helped David Maister self-publish his first book *Managing the Professional Services Firm*. I got to proofread, lay out the book (on a PC with CorelDraw and Adobe PageMaker as I recall), design the cover, and then saw it turn into the world's leading guide to the challenging art of managing a professional services firm. I think at that point I decided to write a book, and I'll always be grateful to David and his amazing wife, Kathy, for setting me on the pathway of consulting and encouraging me to write this book.

There is a whole bunch to this book writing exercise I didn't understand, and I am happy to have found a great team to work with at my publisher Wiley. My great thanks to Mike Campbell for his sponsorship and guidance throughout this process; Christina Verigan, my development editor, for her patient editing; Dawn Kilgore, my managing editor; Susan Geraghty, my copy editor and Sharmila Srinivasan, my content refinement specialist. I also have to thank my friend and fellow author Doug Fletcher for introducing me to Mike and convincing him I was a good bet to make and Ike Williams at Sennott Williams & Rodgers for shepherding me through contracts while he was on a family vacation overseas.

Contributing interviewees make this book great. In alphabetical order, I'd like to thank Graham Anthony, Ray Ausrotas, John Beering, General Paul E. "Gene" Blackwell, Pat Burns, Nancy Lyons Callahan, Marty Curran, Michelle Dennedy, Sheri Dodd, Doug Fletcher, Rob Hays, James Klein, Tom Klenke, Tom Lantzsch, Tom Lattin, Mitch Mongell, Dave Murashige, Athena Murphy, Hunter Reichert, Oliver

Richards, Bob Roda, Don Scales, John Seebeck, Frank Soqui, Sue Spradley, Rick Waldron, and Kevin Watters. Interviewing you was great fun, an amazing learning experience, and I'd do it again in a heartbeat if you'd let me. You are the best of the best and I appreciate you sharing your model with us all. Insider tip: Figure out what companies they all work for and buy stock. I'm imagining my "Grow the Top Line" company index will be one that outperforms the norm (Note: I'm not a broker, and stocks are unreliable – hah!).

There are so many great growth strategists I didn't get a chance to involve in this book. Stay tuned; I hope to be asking for your help on the next one.

Editors are the unsung heroes of all published materials, and a book is the most demanding for that. I have to thank Natalie Barr, my VP of Operations who took the time to read through the manuscript in every form and give me more edits than I ever gave her! I also thank Kim, my wife, and my daughter, Cam, and son, Cole, for that special editing only family can provide, and David Maister for taking the time to provide his always valued guidance as the book took shape, and for giving it a review before I submitted the manuscript. Also my thanks to Tom Klenke, Maria Farrah Howell, and Ray Ausrotas for their review and critique!

One of the things you'll note throughout the book is the references to the Beacon Group. I'm lucky enough to have started Beacon in 2001 with the support of my bride, Kim. We've grown from a first project on a folding table in our kitchen to over 1,500 projects delivered for our global clientele. I've worked at a number of firms and studied hundreds more, which makes me appreciate what we have built. I have the best leadership team I've ever experienced in my career. Our consulting team leadership: Oliver Richards, my Chief Growth Officer and Senior Vice President of Healthcare; Jesse Toronto, my leader of Industrials and M&A Advisory Practices; Mark Heck, my VP of Defense; Andrew Kain, VP Healthcare; Michaela Monahan, VP Healthcare; Lt. Col. Max Kornzen, Director Defense; Dr. Thomas Stuart (PhD), Director Healthcare; Charles "Charlie" Coit, Tech Practice Director; Ganesh Peruvemba, Industrials Director; Ava Gurekian, Associate Director Healthcare; and Logan Pettinato, Associate Director Technology (and my right-hand man). Our operations team leadership: Darren Winslow, VP Finance; Natalie Barr, VP Operations; Carrie Vickers,

Talent Manager; and Adela Smailovic, Marketing Manager. You are all true professionals, and I'm grateful for your contributions to me and the firm every day.

Adela Smailovic deserves special mention. Like the cover? She designed that for me. Our book web page? She did that, too. How about editing the podcast and video interviews? Yes, she led those efforts, too. Thank you Adela for all you do.

Senior staff in the consulting world is only as good as the junior staff that they are working with. At Beacon, we've assembled the most genuinely smart, insightful, caring, and collaborative group of consultants, senior consultants, and managers whom I've ever had the chance to work with. We laugh together, celebrate each other's successes, and help one another when life hits us hard. I am humbled by you and how incredible you all are at what you do. My thanks for making Beacon a part of your journey and for being part of the history of the firm. We've been at this for 20 years, and we just keep getting better thanks to you.

I also need to call out and acknowledge Eliot List. Eliot helped me schedule and transcribe book interviews and assisted in research as needed to support the book. He's been a great part of Beacon and has recently left us to pursue his Fulbright scholarship abroad. I look forward to his future with high expectations.

I've been lucky enough to create a powerful board of directors to keep me on the straight and narrow. Doug Fletcher, Hunter Reichert, and Don Scales: you three are sage, forthright, and pragmatic, perhaps the three best combinations of any board for any firm. I'm thankful you are in my corner.

When you settle in to do something like write a book, you need the support of your family. You don't write a book during normal business hours (at least I didn't). You carve out the time at night and on the weekends, time that you'd normally spend with the people you love. And because they love you back, they let you. Without hesitation. Without a complaint.

Cole Farrah. I've been humbled by your work ethic as I've written this book. You have been a full-time student at Tulane, a comedian, a writer, a producer, director, and an editor of your YouTube channel and your Apple Podcast series. I am grateful that you took these skills and came on board at Beacon to help produce the series of podcasts from the interviews underlying this book. You've unfailingly helped when I've asked for it, and you've grown beyond the man I always dreamed you would be. I love you, Cole, and always will. Stay funny, and I can't wait to see you on SNL or your own series one day. **#PigeonsSaveTheWorld #ColeDoesComedy.**

Cam Farrah. What can't you do? While I was writing this book, you've been a full-time student at Tulane, a proud dog-mom, and working on your Olympic campaign for the full foiling 2024/2028 Nacra 17. You are a force of nature in everything you do, and I appreciate all the support and editing time you gave to me for this book. I love you, Cam, and will be cheering you on forever. Sail fast kid! **#CamSails**

And then there is my bride, Kim. The woman who took my breath away and made my knees knock together when we met. Love at first sight and it just keeps getting better. Whenever I've been in doubt, you've made me strong. Whenever I've hit a roadblock, you've helped me solve it. You told me it was time to start this firm called Beacon. You supported me when I wanted to take the time out in a COVID world to write this book. As Van Morrison said, *"There is no one above you."* I love you.

Index